Roger A Freeman

AMERICAN AIR MUSEUM DUXFORD

A Tribute to American Air Power

American Air Museum Duxford
A Tribute to American Air Power
© 2001 Roger A Freeman
ISBN 1 85780 119 9

Published by Midland Publishing
4 Watling Drive, Hinckley, LE10 3EY, England
Tel: 01455 254 490   Fax: 01455 254 495
E-mail: midlandbooks@compuserve.com

Midland Publishing is an imprint of
Ian Allan Publishing Ltd

Worldwide distribution (except North America):
Midland Counties Publications
4 Watling Drive, Hinckley, LE10 3EY, England
Telephone: 01455 233 747   Fax: 01455 233 737
E-mail: midlandbooks@compuserve.com
www.midlandcountiessuperstore.com

North American trade distribution:
Specialty Press Publishers & Wholesalers Inc.
11605 Kost Dam Road, North Branch, MN 55056
Tel: 651 583 3239   Fax: 651 583 2023
Toll free telephone: 800 895 4585

Design concept and layout
© 2001 Midland Publishing and
Stephen Thompson Associates

Printed in England by
Ian Allan Printing Ltd
Riverdene Business Park, Molesey Road,
Hersham, Surrey, KT12 4RG

Roger A Freeman

AMERICAN AIR MUSEUM DUXFORD

A Tribute to American Air Power

MIDLAND PUBLISHING

Her Majesty the Queen greeting Robert Crawford, Director General Imperial War Museum,
outside the American Air Museum as Ted Inman, Director, Duxford Airfield, looks on.
The Duke of Edinburgh can also be seen meeting other guests at the opening event on
1st August 1997. (DX 97-41-128)

Contents

FOREWORD

The American Air Museum in Britain transformed the Imperial War Museum's branch at Duxford. Through the generosity of thousands of Americans, the support of the Heritage Lottery Fund, the genius of the architect Norman Foster, and the dedication of the team at Duxford, a new standard was set in the presentation and preservation of aircraft. Furthermore, Duxford's public appeal and international reputation were raised to a new level.

Both Roger Freeman and I have been involved in this project since the late 1970s when the seeds which eventually led to it were planted. I am delighted he has written the book to go with the museum, particularly as his reputation stands so high with the many hundreds of American friends I have made during our work on the American Air Museum.

That work continues, as those friends continue their support, making possible new exhibits and improvements to facilities and programmes. I thank them all, and commend Roger's account to date.

Ted Inman

Director, Duxford Airfield IWM

WHY?

On the First of August, nineteen hundred and ninety-seven, Her Majesty Queen Elizabeth II officially opened the American Air Museum in Britain, a £11 million pound building housing the Imperial War Museum's collection of aircraft associated with the armed services of the United States. Present at the Duxford Airfield, Cambridgeshire site were other members of the Royal Family and many well known names in the British and United States establishments. The unenlightened may wonder why a proud nation, so rich in its own aeronautical history, made such an investment acknowledging a great world power. What justifies this tribute to America's air forces? – for an extraordinary tribute it most certainly is.

THE ANSWER

From the early days of manned flight to the present, United States military aviation had many links with the United Kingdom, most notably during the Second World War when at one time more than half the combat strength of the United States Army Air Forces (USAAF) was present. The air offensive pursued by these forces from Britain for the common cause took the lives of nearly thirty thousand young American airmen. Primarily to honour this sacrifice, but also to acknowledge the United States Air Force presence in the following years of international tension generally known as the Cold War, in the late nineteen eighties the Imperial War Museum initiated a project to house its collection of historic American military aircraft and associated artefacts in a purpose built building. The Duxford airfield site was most appropriate as for two years during the Second World War it had been an operational USAAF fighter station. The result is the magnificent American Air Museum in Britain.

This book tells the story of American Air Museum project and the historic links between United States military aviation and Britain that promoted its creation.

Lord Bramall, Chairman of the Imperial War Museum Trustees, presents a framed colour photograph to the Queen of an earlier occasion associated with United States airmen. It depicts the then Princess Elizabeth at the 'christening' ceremony of a B-17 Fortress named *Rose of York* in her honour. Based at Thurleigh near Bedford, this bomber was lost in the North Sea when returning from its 63rd mission, on 3 February 1945. The crew and a BBC reporter with them all perished. (DX 97-41-123)

Following the Opening Ceremony the Queen met many of the Second World War American veterans who had served in Britain. Here she is talking to Robert E Vickers, a former B-24 Liberator pilot, and John E Greenwood, who was a B-17 navigator. Both men are former Presidents of the Eighth Air Force Historical Society, the veterans organisation that has given support to Duxford over many years. (DX 97-38-21)

AMERICAN AIR POWER AND BRITAIN

The 17th December 1903 saw an historic event which man had long dreamed of achieving, powered flight in a heavier than air machine. The place was Kitty Hawk, North Carolina and the two pioneer brothers of manned flight were United States citizens whose forebears of the Wright name came from Kelvedon Hall, Essex, England, two hundred years earlier.

Both air and ground squadrons of the US Army Air Service trained at British establishments during the First World War at some 70 locations. At Harling Road, Norfolk the No 10 Training Depot Station used Avro 504J and K aircraft to give pilot training to US Army personnel. *Via B Robertson*

At that time the armed forces of several nations had already appreciated the advantages of balloons in observing an enemy's deployment. The flying machine suggested a new development: once reliable it might be used for reconnaissance over armies or fleets. Six years were to pass before the US Army purchased a Wright biplane and two more before more aircraft were acquired. However, it was in Europe that the aeroplane was developed apace, significantly so when the leading nations became embroiled in the internecine conflict which later became known as the First World War. The United States became involved from April 1917 and, though quick to muster forces for commitment on the Western Front in Europe, its services relied heavily upon British and French allies for war material, particularly combat aircraft.

Both the US Army and Navy fostered aviation, though chiefly for reconnaissance. There were no suitable indigenous aircraft for the bomber and fighter roles that had developed in Europe, so initially these types were acquired from the allies. Aviation missions were sent to both Britain and France; from the US Army twelve officers and ninety-three men, arrived at Liverpool on 26th June 1917. Having hitherto no pressing incentive to develop its own military aviation, the US Army quickly appreciated that in building a modern force the expertise of its allies should be sought. Negotiations led to an agreement whereby up to 15,000 US Army Air Service personnel would be given ground trade training at British aerodromes, air depots and military schools. By course rotations it is estimated that between June 1917 and March 1919 when training officially terminated some 31,000 US Air Service men served in the UK. The total included 542 cadets who received flying tuition at British establishments. On completion of training most personnel moved to France for operational service. At the time of the Armistice in November 1918 there were 765 officers and 19,307 enlisted men of the US Army Air Service stationed in the UK. In total 211 Aero Squadrons trained in England at one time or another and several of these were actual raised at Royal Flying Corps or Royal Air Force aerodromes. There was a certain degree of integration with British units where Americans served alongside at some 70 airfields in England. In March 1918 two service squadrons, the 137th and 159th, arrived at Duxford to train in maintaining British aircraft, the complement of some 200 men remaining until the end of the war. The last American presence at an RAF airfield was at Wyton where the remaining US Air Service personnel did not leave until early 1920.

Although fewer in numbers, the US Navy airmen sent to the UK included an operational flying unit equipped with Curtiss flying boats that flew North Sea patrols from February 1918. Their base, at Killingholme, Lincolnshire, was taken over by the US Navy the following July when the complement was about 750 officers and men. The US Navy also had an air depot at Eastleigh, near Southampton and five stations in Ireland. The extent of the American presence in their island during hostilities was greater than the average Briton realised; in fact, most did not know there had been US servicemen at Royal Air Force establishments. In those days of restricted transportation GIs were not often seen far from their stations among the civilian population.

Co-operation with the RAF inevitably led to the American aviators stationed in Europe being much influenced by the British service. Not only was there a strong body of opinion among American air officers that military aviation in the US should, like the RAF, be a separate service, but also that in any future conflict bombing aircraft would play a decisive part in the outcome through taking the battle to the enemy's war infrastructure. The bomber could reach strategic objectives and destroy armaments factories and associated war production in the enemy homeland.

Major General Hugh Trenchard of the RAF, an advocate of strategic bombing formed the Independent Force in 1918 which mounted a campaign of operations against targets in Germany. The US Army Air Service's commander in France, General William Mitchell, impressed by Trenchard's endeavours, took every opportunity to proclaim the prowess of the bomber on his return to the USA. The Glenn Martin company had produced a worthy twin-engine biplane bomber to meet Army Air Service requirements and in July 1920 Mitchell used such bombers to demonstrate the potential of aerial bombing. Selected warships taken from Germany in reparations, anchored off Virginia Capes, were sunk by Mitchell's bombers, much to the chagrin of US Navy admirals. Mitchell was equally unpopular with many in the Army hierarchy who were want to see military aircraft only as machines to support the ground forces. Mitchell's continued and uncautioned promotion of an independent role for air power eventually led to his court martial and demotion. Nevertheless, his objectives were also held by other senior officers in the Air Service who, more guardedly, continued to pursue the same goals without incurring the displeasure of the Army old guard. A more substantiated position for the Army's air element was established in July 1926 when the Air Service became the Air Corps.

The early post-war years saw the spending on military aviation severely reduced in both America and Britain. The United States turned to isolationism while Britain, having suffered huge casualties and loss of wealth, took on an anti-war stance. Few orders were forthcoming for new aircraft types although in America the US Army continued to provide funds for experimental advancement. While the western allies had imposed conditions on Germany forbidding development of military aviation, that nation had nonetheless become one of the most air-minded in the world. When these restrictions became only loosely monitored a competent German aviation industry blossomed, with civil aircraft output soon turned to military types by the Nazi administration.

At first Britain and France could not accept that Hitler would take Germany into another war. Belatedly some re-armament was undertaken but by then, in many aviation developments, German companies had a lead, fuelled by state expenditure. Appreciating their own weaknesses both Britain and France turned to American aircraft manufacturers for purchases during the late nineteen-thirties. If the United States government still pursued an isolationist policy and limited its military and naval expenditure to defence, the vast distances from one continental city to another had promoted the airliner as a quick means of transport. In supplying this market aircraft manufacturers made advances in airframe design and manufacture as well as in some types of aero-

engines. Before the outbreak of war the RAF had ordered the Harvard trainer from North American Aviation, the Hudson general reconnaissance bomber from Lockheed and the Catalina flying boat from Consolidated.

The US Army generally ordered new military aircraft on the results of competitive trials conducted by its Air Corps experimental establishment at Wright Field, Dayton, Ohio. In 1934 it issued what was known as a circular letter to manufacturers inviting submissions for a new bomber to replace the type currently in service. Finding no stipulation on the number of engines required to power the design, the Boeing company used four whereas other competitors' designs had two, the norm expected by the Air Corps. The resulting Boeing Model 299 was the world's first all-metal, four-engine bomber and, despite the crash of the prototype in the later stages of testing, easily won the competition. Eventually designated B-17 and called Flying Fortress, initially 13 were ordered for trials. Isolationist elements of government and the US Navy saw no reason for this far ranging bomber. However, albeit among themselves, Air Corps enthusiasts for strategic bombing saw the B-17 as the vehicle which could be used to further their endeavours. By installing turbo-supercharged engines, a self-regulating crew oxygen system and a very advanced and accurate bombsight, the B-17 could attack targets from the sub-stratosphere; an optimum 25,000 feet being twice the height at which bombers then in service were expected to operate.

Thus a doctrine of daylight high-altitude precision bombing was fostered by the Air Corps and eventually given substance by a change in government policy. The Roosevelt administration, whose enlightened president realised that America must re-arm to meet the hostile dictatorial regimes threatening world peace, began to invest vast sums in military aviation. With Europe at war, new types were ordered into production 'straight off the drawing board' and by the spring of 1941 financial appropriations for air power were more that two billion dollars, 36 times that of 1937.

Top: Mechanics service a Duxford-based Thunderbolt on a fine summer day in 1944, but more often the task had to be performed in inclement weather with no protection. The majority of US Army Air Forces' personnel in the United Kingdom served in a support role, approximately twenty men on the ground to every one in the air.

Above left: The common form of transport in wartime Britain was the pedal cycle and most American servicemen soon acquired a personal 'bike'.

Above right: Winter was a particularly hard time for ground crews working long hours both day and night to keep aircraft airworthy. Temperatures may not have been extreme but GIs found the cold very penetrating.

THE SECOND WORLD WAR

With the overrunning of Western Europe in 1940 Britain took over most of the outstanding French and Belgian orders for aircraft, although payment was becoming a problem with large orders being placed in the USA for aircraft. While still officially neutral, the United States was by then clearly supportive of Britain.

After several hours confined in a noise deafening, vibrating aircraft at altitudes where the temperature was below zero and oxygen intake essential, it was a great release to be back on the ground. A cigarette to fight off the fatigue while the ground crew ask how the day went.

Later that year, easing the financial problem, the Roosevelt government introduced Lend-Lease help to nations deemed critical to the defence of the United States which covered most British needs for war equipment and munitions. Simply, it was what its title indicates, lending and leasing of the required materials. Lend-Lease enabled Britain to acquire more than 20,000 aircraft from United States manufacturers during the next five years, with a score of different types entering operational service with the RAF and Fleet Air Arm. In return Britain entrusted the American authorities with much of its secret experimental work including radar and jet-propulsion. Intelligence matters and operational expertise were also provided from the British side. US Army Air Corps officers clad in civilian attire came to the UK to observe the air war, while other personnel oversaw the delivery and assembly of aircraft.

Filled with the spirit of adventure and championing the cause of freedom, many young citizens of the United States wanted to fly with the RAF. This they could only do legally by first going to Canada and enlisting in the Royal Canadian Air Force. Aircrew volunteers from any nation were welcomed but the British government underlined American support by allowing the RAF to form special fighter squadrons with all-American pilot complements called Eagle Squadrons. In addition to boosting the strength of RAF Fighter Command, they provided useful propaganda to advance Britain's cause in the USA and show enemy nations where America's sympathies lay. However, far more US subjects served with RAF Bomber and Coastal Commands than the three Eagle Squadrons, many preferring to stay with the British service long after their own nation became involved in hostilities.

On 7 December 1941 the Japanese attacked Pearl Harbor, Hawaii and two days later Germany and Italy declared war on the United States. A 'beat Germany first' policy was established between the United States, Britain and other Allies, and to this end the US Army Air Forces (a semi-autonomous advance on the Army Air Corps, created in June 1941) would take part in the air campaign over western Europe. Early planning centred on air support for a cross-Channel invasion of continental Europe in the late summer of 1942. This was soon seen

The US government's Lend-Lease act of 1941 provided Britain with much needed war equipment. Many types of aircraft included early Boeing B-17s which in RAF service became Fortress Is. These, then giants, provoked much interest amongst RAF personnel.

as unrealistic at that stage of the war and attention then turned to a build-up for landings in north-west Africa, Operation TORCH, to be staged later that year. However, the advocates of daylight precision bombardment were eager to put their doctrine to practical test and a heavy bomber element was prepared for deployment in Britain. The industrial heart of Germany was well within range of bombers based in England, providing an ideal objective for a strategic campaign.

The scale of the USAAF commitment to the UK was extraordinary. In January 1942 the British were notified that airfields for 320 bomber, 37 fighter, 32 transport and 18 reconnaissance squadrons would be required for a total of some 7,000 combat aircraft. The figure was to be frequently reviewed and amended but meeting the demand for airfields entailed the biggest civil engineering programme ever undertaken in Britain. Each new bomber airfield, built to the Class A standard already established for RAF Bomber Command, featured three converging concrete runways and by the summer 1942 it was established that one USAAF bomber group of four squadrons would be stationed at each. This meant that 75 Class A airfields had to be found or built in the greater East Anglian area where the American bombers were to be deployed. Airfields to the same standard also had to be provided for the transports and sites in the Salisbury Plain area were initially allocated. Fighters were generally to be based on grass surfaced airfields and most of these already existed. Despite the fluctuations in force planning, some 130 airfields were allocated for USAAF use at this time.

An advance party of USAAF officers arrived in the UK early in February 1942. Other details soon followed and headquarters were set up at Bushy Park, Teddington for the US Eighth Air Force. The Eighth was the first US offensive air force, numbers One to Seven being those in the continental USA and overseas dependencies. Major General Carl Spaatz assumed command, while the VIII Bomber Command set up at High Wycombe, close to RAF Bomber Command HQ, was headed by Brigadier General Ira Eaker. The first flying unit to arrive, the 15th Bombardment Squadron, was to have been converted by the RAF for a night-fighter role with airborne searchlight-equipped aircraft. This technique was abandoned

Several hundred US citizens volunteered for service with British and Commonwealth forces before their nation became involved in Second World War hostilities. The most famous were the so-called Eagle Squadron fighter pilots, although many men flew with RAF Bomber Command. Two successful fighter pilots were Gus Daymond and Chesley Peterson of No 71 Squadron (seen on the right) who were credited with eight and seven air victories, respectively. (CH 3735)

and instead the unit trained in light bomber operations with an RAF squadron. The first USAAF offensive operation from Britain took place on 4 July 1942 when six crews, flying RAF Bostons, took part in a joint low-level attack on airfields in Holland. Two American crewed aircraft failed to return from what was primarily a flag waving event for Independence Day. USAAF fighter squadrons equipped with Spitfires were entering operations at this time, tutored by RAF squadrons and flying under RAF Fighter Command control.

The first Eighth Air Force heavy bomber combat mission was not flown until 17 August 1942 when 12 B-17Es of the 97th Bomb Group bombed rail marshalling yards at Rouen. A group was the basic operational unit in the USAAF, its assigned squadrons subservient and flying as a team. By late October 1942 the USAAF had four B-17 Fortress groups, one with B-24 Liberators, three with Spitfires and one with P-38 Lightnings operational. Another four heavy bomber, three transport, two medium bomber, two fighter and a reconnaissance group had also reached Britain, the majority being assigned to the newly formed Twelfth Air Force to support the TORCH landings. This, taking place in early November, denuded the Eighth Air Force of all but six bomber and one fighter group, the former mostly newcomers. However, the Eighth Air Force was now committed to a strategic role under General Eaker, pioneering daylight precision bombing. Unfortunately the contingencies of other war fronts saw planned expansion delayed until the following spring and its full force could not be achieved for another year.

No more Liberator groups were received by the Eighth until the summer of 1943 and those on hand were often diverted to other tasks and the Mediterranean Theatre of War. The Fortress groups carried the main weight of the Eighth's campaign for nearly a year flying unescorted raids ever deeper into enemy held airspace. A combined bomber offensive set up with the RAF in the spring of 1943 listed priority targets for strategic attack, neutralisation of the enemy air force being a pre-requisite. To this end aircraft industry targets were frequent objectives for the bombers which met stiffening resistance from the defences and increasingly heavy loses. Some of

The first USAAF bombing mission in the European Theatre of Operations took place on 4 July 1942 using Bostons borrowed from the RAF. It was a costly enterprise as two of the American crews failed to return and the leader's aircraft was a badly shot up. For his conduct that day Major Charles Kegelman (far right) was awarded a Distinguished Service Cross and the three other members of his crew, left to right, T/Sgt R L Golay, Sgt B B Cunningham and 2nd Lt R M Dorton all received the Distinguished Flying Cross. This pose for the press occurred after the award ceremony. Before USAAF operations from the UK ceased more than 300 DSC and over 50,000 DFC awards were made. The Medal of Honor, highest US decoration for bravery, was won by 16 airmen based in Britain, half the USAAF recipients in the Second World War.

The wounded ball-turret gunner of the 94th Bomb Group Fortress named *Hard To Get* being lowered through the right waist window after the mission to Kiel on 13 December 1943. Some 28,000 American airmen lost their lives flying from British bases and another 8,000 were wounded or injured. (EA10281)

Leaders of the strategic bombing campaign against Nazi
Germany, Air Chief Marshall Sir Arthur Harris, C in C RAF Bomber
Command, and Major General Ira Eaker, CG US Eighth Air Force,
take the salute at an awards ceremony march past in 1943.
Co-operation between British and American forces was good
throughout the war.

the fiercest and most concentrated air battles in history
took place between the Fortress formations and intercepting enemy fighters. By the autumn losses and battle
damage had the campaign in crisis. If daylight raids were
to continue long range fighter escort had to be provided;
this was in hand.

The fighter element of the USAAF sent to Britain in
1942 was primarily for defensive purposes. Although the
self-defending bomber concept still held sway the provision of fighter escort for the B-17s and B-24s was seen as
an asset and by the spring of the following year a neces-
sity. Three groups equipped with P-47 Thunderbolts,
more than 200 aircraft, became operational in April 1943
but their radius of action was only some 200 miles. Mea-
sures were taken to install jettisonable auxiliary tanks
and devise a means of pressurising them so that fuel
could be drawn at high altitude. First used in August they
enabled Thunderbolts to reach the German border and
offer a good measure of protection for the bombers.
Later, by carrying larger 'drop tanks' the radius of action
was pushed out to 350 miles. Meanwhile the Luftwaffe
was increasing its defensive strength and improving tactics, taking an increasing toll of the bombers in the areas
beyond American fighter support.

Twin-engine P-38 Lightnings introduced to further
bomber escorts, were to be handicapped by technical
difficulties. P-51 Mustangs, entering operations in
December 1943, proved to be the fighter that the Eighth
Air Force had been seeking in that their internal fuel load
gave a radius of action of near 400 miles, and with jettisonable tanks they could fly to any target the bombers
could visit. The Eighth eventually equipped or converted
all but one of its 15 fighter groups to Mustangs. As the
American fighter escort force expanded so its success
against the Luftwaffe advanced. The attrition suffered by
the Luftwaffe fighter arm reached a point during the
early spring of 1944 where air superiority was firmly held
by Lightning, Thunderbolt and Mustang pilots. In this
achievement Ninth Air Force fighters also played a significant part, albeit that their task was primarily tactical.

In the spring of 1943 the Eighth Air Force commenced
operations with B-26 Marauder medium bombers. After
a disastrous raid flown at low-level the Marauders were
transferred to VIII Air Support Command, thereafter
operating successfully at medium altitudes against
short-range targets. VIII Air Support Command's main
mission was to co-operate with ground forces.

Lt. General James Doolittle, commanding the Eighth Air Force,
Lt. General Carl Spaatz who headed the overall American bomber
headquarters, United States Strategic Air Forces in Europe, and
Major General Frederick L Anderson, chief of Eighth Air Force
operations, attending the 100th mission party of the 96th Bomb
Group at Snetterton Heath, Norfolk on 1 April 1944. The 96th had
more B-17s destroyed by enemy action than any other group flying from England. (EA18999)

In 1943 a Wings for Victory savings campaign in Bermondsey, London raised £800,000 for the purchase of aircraft. A decision was made to 'buy' four Flying Fortresses as a gesture of Anglo-American goodwill. One of the B-17s was named *Rotherhithe's Revenge* for the most heavily 'blitzed' borough in the capital. Christened on 16 February 1944 by the Chairman of the Bermondsey War Savings Committee using a bottle of Thames river water, the bomber went on to survive hostilities with 122 missions to its credit. Note that the wartime censor has used his red pen to obscure any unit patches, badges etc that might have given a clue as to which USAAF operational units were in the country. (USAAC23)

P-38 Lightnings of the Ninth Air Force's 370th Fighter Group attacking enemy positions at St Malo, 17 August 1944. Low-level bombing and strafing attacks in support of ground forces brought heavy losses to Eighth and Ninth Air Force fighters in the weeks following the invasion of Normandy. (KY34475)

A C-47 of the 435th Troop Carrier Group with two Waco assault gliders in tow. These unarmed transports suffered grievously during most operations involving the delivery of paratroops and supply drops. The reliable military version of the Douglas DC-3 airliner played the major air transport role in support of the Allied land campaigns in north-west Europe, 1944-45. In the summer of 1944 there were over a thousand based in Britain.

P-47 Thunderbolts of the 78th Fighter Group take off from Duxford on a bomber escort mission, summer 1944.
The American long-range fighters flying from Britain were primarily responsible for achieving and maintaining air superiority in enemy airspace, a major contribution to victory.

B-26 Marauder medium bombers on their way to strike targets in the Cherbourg peninsula on D-Day, 6 June 1944. For several weeks during the winter of 1943-44 and following spring these Ninth Air Force bombers flew missions to attack the V-weapon sites in the Pas de Calais. Their contribution to this campaign undoubtedly reduced the enemy's capability to launch these weapons against London.

In October 1943 this command with its four operational B-26 Marauder groups and other tactical flying units was redesignated as the US Ninth Air Force and given a support role for the forthcoming cross-Channel invasion. Ninth Air Force expansion was rapid during the winter of 1943-44, as was that of the Eighth Air Force. Another development during the autumn of 1943 was the establishment of the US Fifteenth Air Force in the Allied occupied area of southern Italy. The Fifteenth was composed of the eight heavy bomber groups already in the Mediterranean theatre of war and the diversion of 15 new groups being trained for the Eighth Air Force. However, the Eighth Air Force HQ in England was later redes-

ignated as the United States Strategic Air Forces in Europe (USSTAF) and had operational control over both the Eighth and Fifteenth Air Forces – the new Eighth Air Force HQ was the former VIII Bomber Command HQ which it absorbed. James Doolittle replaced Ira Eaker as Commanding General of the Eighth and Lt General Spaatz at USSTAF remained the senior USAAF commander in Europe.

By the date of Operation OVERLORD, the invasion of Normandy, the Ninth Air Force had 21 fighter, 11 bomber, 14 troop carrier and two reconnaissance groups with over 5,000 aircraft. The Eighth also had some 5,000 aircraft with 41 bomber, 15 fighter and two reconnaissance groups, the last heavy bomber group starting operations on D-Day, 6 June 1944. The personnel strength of the USAAF in the UK stood at 436,417 at this time, soon to diminish as the Ninth Air Force moved to liberated France. The Eighth Air Force, apart from temporary detachments, remained in Britain to the end of hostilities.

During the war's final year the Eighth Air Force was frequently diverted from its strategic campaign to partici-

pate in tactical missions in support of the Allied armies. Even so, it was during this period that the enemy's war industry was subjected to heaviest attack, with particular success against the sources of petroleum production. German output fell by 90 per cent between May 1944 and March 1945. Seventy-two per cent of the bombs dropped on Germany were delivered after the Normandy invasion. A diversion from offensive objectives for both Eighth and Ninth Air Force bombers during the winter of 1943-44 and following spring were the attacks on V-weapon sites. An effort to help minimise the bombardment of London and south-east England by 'flying bombs' and rockets.

While the primary task of the Eighth's fighters was protecting the bombers, from January 1944 they were allowed and encouraged to participate in strafing attacks on enemy ground targets, mostly airfields. Eventually the Mustangs and Thunderbolts became an additional offensive force with specific strafing objectives, highly dangerous but effective, particularly against rail traffic. Most of the steel and impregnated paper jettisonable tanks used by fighters were made in Britain.

In operations from Britain during the Second World War some 32,000 US airmen were killed in action or on active service, mostly USAAF personnel but including those from the US Navy flying oceanic patrols from west country bases. Approximately 27,000 of these were Eighth Air Force men, this force having a total casualty figure of some 47,000 which included 18,000 prisoners of war. In total more than 12,000 aircraft of the Eighth and Ninth Air Force were missing in action, destroyed in accidents flying from the UK or scrapped due to damage sustained.

With victory in Europe, VE-Day, the Eighth Air Force bomber units were quickly redeployed, the majority having returned to the USA by July 1945. Most fighter units remained until the early autumn as ground forces had priority in trans-Atlantic shipping. The last combat associated elements of the USAAF withdrew from Honington airfield, Suffolk in February 1946 and from the large air depot at Burtonwood the following May.

Opposite page: The wedding at Quidenham parish church, Norfolk, of a sergeant from nearby Snetterton Heath airfield and his English fiancée. Some 60,000 British girls married American servicemen during or shortly after the Second World War and several thousand more during the Cold War.

This page:

While the scale of America's provisions for its ally could not be matched, where possible the hard-pressed British nation did its best to reciprocate in many ways. Ground crew men of Mustang *Nancy V* take a welcome hot drink from a Church Army Mobile Canteen, manned by local women, on a chill winter's day. The auxiliary fuel tanks under the wing of this fighter at Bodney, Norfolk, were manufactured in the UK.

American servicemen were popular with British children, not only as a source of confectionery and other rarely seen luxuries, but because they did not patronise. Christmas parties at local USAAF bases were never to be forgotten experiences for youngsters. Many of the toys and other gifts had been made by the service-men during their spare time.

A drink with the girls. GIs complained that England's beer was warm and weak but this did not stop many becoming partial to it. Public houses were popular locations for 'off base' visits. As American film stars were heart-throbs for many British girls, the arrival of the GIs was Hollywood come to life

THE COLD WAR

A massive and hurried demobilisation of what had been to a large degree an American citizen's army took place in 1946, the USAAF being quickly reduced to a score of combat units. However, the achievements of airpower during the Second World War, plus the deterrent posed by atomic weapons – delivery being dependent on the heavy bomber during the immediate post-war years – finally led to the creation of the fully autonomous US Air Force in September 1947: blue uniforms gradually replacing khaki.

The Nazi menace and Japanese imperialism having been defeated, an era of peace was anticipated. But another dictatorial regime began to cloud the promise, the Berlin blockade of 1948 making plain the Soviet Union leaders' hostility towards the West. In that year B-29 Superfortresses were deployed in Britain and work put in hand to ready the only three airfields then capable of handling these large aircraft comfortably, Marham, Lakenheath and Sculthorpe. The United States believed the threat of the atom bomb would caution the Soviets against any aggressive action. Thus began a regular cycle of 30 days temporary duty for Strategic Air Command (SAC) B-29 groups in England with the 3rd Air Division as the local controlling headquarters. Work was soon put in hand to enlarge other airfields with the 3,000 yard runways desirable for these large aircraft. The Americans also returned, in May 1948, to Burtonwood which became a major depot for the US military.

In the autumn of 1944 USSTAF had moved from London to a site near Paris and later that year, following its redesignation as United States Air Forces in Europe (USAFE), to Germany. Within two years the command could only show some three dozen combat aircraft as on operational status at its airfields. The Berlin blockade, followed by the communist take-over of Czechoslovakia, brought mounting concern in western governments about Soviet intentions. This led, in April 1949, to the United States and eleven European nations signing a mutual defence treaty to meet any attack from the east. The North Atlantic Treaty Organisation (NATO) was to foster re-armament to meet the Soviet treat, only to suffer some delay through the outbreak of the Korean War the following year. USAFE became a major element of the NATO air forces and established several of its bases in the UK. The 3rd Air Division, which had overseen SAC activities in Britain since May 1948, was reassigned to USAFE in January 1951 and this Headquarters at South Ruislip was upgraded to become the 3rd Air Force at the beginning of May to meet plans for a substantial number of combat aircraft to be based in Britain. The first of these, the 81st Fighter Interceptor Wing with three squadrons, moved into Bentwaters and Shepherds Grove airfield in August that year. This wing was equipped with F-86A

Sabres, the high performance swept wing jet, was then the only operational fighter in the Western camp capable of dealing with the Soviet MiG-15. Initially the primary mission of the 81st was defence of UK air bases. Later that year a fighter-bomber wing arrived at Manston with F-84E Thunderjets and in June 1952 the 20th Fighter Bomber Wing, which would have tactical nuclear weapon delivery capability, took up station at Wethersfield. In the same month B-45 Tornado light bombers, also with nuclear weapons capability, began to arrive at Sculthorpe.

Meanwhile SAC temporary deployments to the UK continued, with airfields at Greenham Common, Brize Norton and Fairford being enlarged for use by B-29 and B-50 Superfortresses and derivatives. Giant Convair six-engined B-36s also made occasional deployments to the UK from January 1951. The first all-jet bombers entered SAC service later that year but their first UK deployment did not occur until June 1953 when the 306th Bomb Wing brought 15 B-47s to Fairford. From then on units with this type replaced the Superfortresses on 90 day temporary duty at the British SAC bases. The peak period of both the USAF's aircraft and personal strength in the UK was 1954-55.

Following the inauguration of NATO came the Mutual Air Defence Pact (MADP) which for the RAF and Royal Navy meant American funded new aircraft, advanced electronic equipment and early warning radars. For Britain this included 52 Neptune maritime patrol aircraft, 430 F-86 Sabres built in Canada with US dollars, and Washington (basic Boeing B-29) bombers to fill the gap between outgoing Lincolns and incoming jet-engined Canberras. When in service the Canberra proved so outstanding that it was put into production by Martin for the USAF as their B-57. For the Royal Navy under MDAP came Douglas Skyraider early warning aircraft and Grumman Avengers in the anti-submarine role. Later, in turn, the Royal Navy was able to introduce, by cross-carrier operating, the US Navy to angled decks and mirror landing systems. From 1966 the RAF has relied on Lockheed Hercules (USAF C-130) as its main heavy transport and this fleet was supplemented by an updated version at the end of the century.

USAF build-up in the UK continued until the mid-nineteen fifties with a total of 13 occupied airfields and 10 others prepared for use should the Cold War suddenly become hot. Bentwaters, Sculthorpe, Wethersfield, Woodbridge and Manston were the main operational bases for USAFE's 3rd Air Force, while Lakenheath, Brize Norton, Upper Heyford, Fairford and Greenham Common served SAC. Rationalisation during 1958 saw USAFE inactivate the fighter wing at Manston, the airfield then being returned to the RAF. However, following disagreement with the French over atomic-capable units based in their country USAFE had to withdraw these from France, the 10th Tactical Reconnaissance Wing going to Alconbury and the 48th Tactical Fighter Wing to Lakenheath, the latter arriving in January 1960. With the tactical fighter able to out-perform the current tactical light bomber, in 1962 the 47th Bomb Wing at Sculthorpe was inactivated and its B-66 Destroyers withdrawn. USAFE's only in-flight refuelling squadron at the same base soon suffered the same fate. This and other little used installations including those prepared for emergency use were relinquished during the next two years and the closure of Thor missile sites began. These reductions due to an overall reduction in USAF facilities world-wide and the increase in destructive potential of new weapon systems that allowed economies of scale.

Since coming to the UK in the early nineteen fifties the 20th and 81st Wings had been equipped with a succession of fighter types, Sabres, Thunderjets, Super Sabres, Voodoos and Phantoms. In 1970 the 20th Wing converted from Super Sabres to the F-111 swing-wing aircraft which, more bomber than fighter, had a range that could take it into western Russia. The 48th Wing at Lakenheath was also re-equipped with 'F One Elevens' seven years later and at the end of that decade the 81st Wing received the A-10 ground attack aircraft, unofficially known as the Warthog due to its ungainly appearance. In 1982, as a counter to the Soviet's deployment of medium-range ground launched missiles in eastern Europe, the USAFE formed a wing at Greenham Common to receive the Tomahawk cruise missiles. A second cruise missile wing, raised at Molesworth late in 1986, was short lived as a year later President Reagan and Soviet leader Gorbachev signed an agreement to remove intermediate range ground-launched missiles from Europe.

Thereafter a mellowing of east-west relations heralded a major reduction in the USAF presence in Britain, but not before contingents from Alconbury, Lakenheath and Upper Heyford had been detached to take part in offensive operations over Iraq in the Desert Storm conflict of winter 1990-91. Eighth Air Force B-52 Stratofortresses flew bombing missions from Fairford against Iraq during this campaign, and again eight years later for raids on Serbia/Kosovo. However, the first offensive bombing sorties flown from the UK since the Second World War were conducted by 18 F-111s from Lakenheath against Libyan targets on 15 April 1986 as reprisals for a spate of terrorist attacks in Europe instigated by the Gadaffi regime.

In August 1951 the 81st Fighter Interceptor Wing, equipped with the first swept wing fighters to see service in the UK, was deployed in East Anglia to protect USAF bomber bases. The F-86A Sabres first arrived at Shepherds Grove, Suffolk.
Via G Pennick

First USAF formation to be 'permanently' based in the UK in support of the NATO mission was the 20th Fighter Bomber Wing which took up station at Wethersfield, Essex in the summer of 1952. Its F-84G Thunderjets could be equipped with tactical nuclear weapons and this deterrent was maintained through re-equipment with F-100 and F-111, the last type being flown from Upper Heyford. All told, the 20th Wing spent over forty years in the UK.

1941 'EAGLE BOYS' FLYING AGAIN

Now Among the World's First Jet Aces Trailing MIGs in Korea

From NOEL MONKS

Tokio, Sunday.

AMERICAN pilots who paid their fares to London in 1941 and fought alongside the R.A.F. in their volunteer Eagle Squadron, are among the world's jet aces in Korea. Many of them have streak... ...aces in and they have not the same bo... ...ir hair, into the cockpits of R.A.F. Hurr... ...mbed

With the end of the Cold War NATO's mission was revised to provide military help or force to meet crisis situations that might arise in Europe and Asia Minor. The United States continued to shoulder the major contribution, but there was no longer need for the extensive commitment that had been in place to meet the Soviet threat. Between 1991 and 1995 the USAF inactivated or moved all units from Alconbury, Bentwaters, Upper Heyford and Woodbridge with the closure of these stations. Both the 20th and 81st Wings had 42 years continuous service in Britain. By the end of the century USAF flight activity was concentrated at Mildenhall and Lakenheath. Mildenhall still holds 3rd Air Force HQ and acts as the main air terminal for trans-Atlantic traffic. Also stationed there are the 100th Air Refueling Wing and the 352nd Special Operations Group, the former equipped with venerable KC-135 tankers providing air refuelling for NATO air forces, and the latter with a variety of helicopters and transports on call for special operations. Lakenheath is the only American combat strike base remaining in the UK with F-15 Eagle and Strike Eagle aircraft.

Throughout the USAF's presence in the UK many of its units have been involved in humanitarian assistance in Europe and the Middle East. Notable assistance rendered in Britain was during the east coast flooding of January 1953 (17 of the 307 people killed were Americans) and oil

The swept wing F-84F Thunderstreak replaced the Bentwaters Sabres in 1954 giving that base a tactical nuclear weapon capability. JATO rockets for use in short field take-offs were demonstrated but otherwise rarely used. *Via G Pennick*

Opposite page top: The US Third Air Force had its largest complement of combat aircraft in the mid 1950s. This demonstration of in-flight refuelling involved a KB-50J tanker of the 420th Air Refueling Squadron at Sculthorpe, Norfolk, a twin-jet B-66B Destroyer tactical bomber from the same base, a Wethersfield F-100 Super Sabre of the 20th Tactical Fighter Wing feeding from the left wing, and a Bentwaters F-101 Voodoo off the right wing. *G Pennick*

Opposite page bottom: Arrival of F-101 Voodoos at Bentwaters, April 1958. For eight years the 81st Tactical Fighter Wing was the only wing in USAFE operating this powerful aircraft in the fighter bomber role. Its main advantage over the F-100 was in range. *Via G Pennick*

slick clean-up operations following the *Torrey Canyon* shipping disaster of April 1967. USAF personnel serving long periods at UK installations were permitted to bring their families and house them in the area. Local economies benefited from this presence, not only through enhanced commerce but because many British civilians found employment at US bases.

Top left and top right: With some opposition to American military bases on British soil in peacetime, the USAF made public relations an important issue. Local civil administrators were invited to visit the American airfields and several were given flights. The man in full flight gear is Sir Stuart S Mallinson, Lord Lieutenant of Essex, photographed before a trip in a two-seat F-100F. Seeing him settled in is the Wethersfield CO at the time, June 1957, Colonel Raymond Toliver. In the same year members of the Deben, Suffolk Urban District Council were given flights from Bentwaters in the base T-33A. *Via G Pennick*

Above: Popular with the British and good for public relations were the annual 'Open House' events at the major airfields. People were permitted to enter the Colonel's 'run about', a veteran Douglas C-47 of the Second World War, at the Bentwaters show on 11 May 1963. *Via G Pennick*

Mildenhall hosted the Third Air Force HQ and became the main USAF transport terminal in the UK. Before the advent of the big jets the C-124 Globemaster II was the giant of the skies. This one, belonging to the 63rd Troop Carrier Wing, had just disgorged the 42 piece USAF in Europe Band on an August day, 1964. *Via G Pennick*

The F-100D Super Sabre was the main workhorse of the tactical fighter squadrons during the 1960s, with some 75 based at both Lakenheath and Bentwaters. The 48th Tactical Fighter Wing at Lakenheath flew the type for 16 years. *G Pennick*

Sharing Woodbridge with the 81st TFW was the 67th Aerospace Recovery and Rescue Squadron operating helicopters. Apart from the obvious mission it undertook special operations and in 1988 metamorphosed into a new unit charged exclusively with clandestine tasks. This is an HH-53C of 1972. *G Pennick*

The versatile F-4 Phantom replaced Bentwaters Voodoos and Lakenheath Super Sabres in the tactical fighter-bomber role. These two are on approach to Bentwaters, September 1970. *G Pennick*

Although Alconbury units supplied the reconnaissance requirements of the Third Air Force, as this role diminished due to satellite and other forms of intelligence gathering, the 10th Tactical Reconnaissance Wing took over two of the 'tank busting' A-10 squadrons from the 81st TFW. The nose end of Colonel James C. Evans personal A-10A was, typically, festooned with instructional data and insignia. *G Pennick*

A B-52 Stratofortress taxis out for take-off at Fairford. This cotswold airfield has been the main base for USAF heavy bomber operations since the 1980s. Stratofortresses flew bombing missions from Fairford during both the Gulf and Kosovo hostilities. *I Mactaggart*

THE MUSEUM – Finding the Finance

The Imperial War Museum was established by Act of Parliament in 1920. Its purpose is to collect, preserve and display material and information connected with military operations in which Britain or the Commonwealth have been involved since August 1914. Duxford Airfield is a branch of the Imperial War Museum and, though geographically distant from the headquarters in Lambeth Road, London, it is nevertheless an integral part of the Museum which is ideal for the display of large exhibits. Duxford is also the main storage site for archive, film, photographs, books and documents.

Famous film star James Stewart poses with Charlton Heston, Sir John Grandy and HRH The Duke of Kent, at the Los Angeles fund raising dinner in 1992. It was Stewart who proposed Charlton Heston as US campaign chairman after John Tower was killed. Stewart flew B-24 Liberators in combat from England on 22 missions while serving with the Eighth Air Force.

It is highly appropriate for a section of the Imperial War Museum to be based at an historic fighter station such as Duxford. Duxford's service career spanned two World Wars. It played an important role in the Battle of Britain and much of the airfield is preserved as it was during the early 1940s.

Duxford airfield, opened in 1917 as a flying training station, was later home to RAF fighter squadrons in the years of uneasy peace. It played a significant part during the Battle of Britain and then housed the Air Fighting Development Unit that also evaluated captured enemy aircraft. One of the first USAAF units to be based in the UK, the 350th Fighter Group, arrived on 4 October 1942, and later, in April 1943, the 78th Fighter Group took up residence and stayed until the end of the war.

At the end of the Second World War Duxford Airfield was handed back to the RAF and once again became an air defence fighter station. By 1961 the runway was considered to be too short and the airfield too far from the coast to fulfil this role any longer. Duxford Airfield was formally closed in 1968. For some years afterwards various schemes were put forward for its conversion but none of these came to anything and the site became derelict. Then, in 1976, the Imperial War Museum took it on because of its suitability for the storage of large exhibits and the story of The Imperial War Museum Duxford began.

A huge amount of work was required to turn the airfield into a Museum, but the effort was worthwhile because not only was there space for expansion but also, through an agreement with Cambridgeshire County Council, the operational status of the airfield was restored. This encouraged owners and operators of historic aircraft to come to Duxford. The site would primarily display the aircraft collection, which could now be increased through new acquisitions, with a priority for types operational during the Second World War which were now becoming increasingly scarce.

An important aspect of the growth of the collection's growth was the addition of many historic American combat examples. The first to be restored at Duxford was the P-51 Mustang, now on display at the Museum's Headquarters in Lambeth Road, London. Next the B-17 was

obtained, followed by a steady stream of examples donated by the US Air Force such as the F-100 and a B-29 which was recovered from the California desert in 1980.

In the early 1970s Lt Colonel John Woolnough, a B-24 Liberator pilot during the war, had formed a veterans' association in the United States, the 8th Air Force Historical Society. Over the next ten years Society membership grew to some 20,000, making the Society one of the largest of its kind in the United States. John Woolnough was eager to support Duxford's plans for a tribute to all those Americans who served out of British bases during the Second World War and a memorial to the 30,000 who gave their lives, and in 1977 the 8th Air Force Memorial

Colonel John Doolittle unveils the bust of his father, the famous airman James H Doolittle who was one of the Eighth Air Force commanding generals. John Doolittle flew B-26 Marauders in North Africa during the Second World War. The bust is now in the American Air Museum. (Berliner 41587-21)

and Museum Foundation (8AFMMF) was formed as an adjunct of the 8th Air Force Historical Society to support activities perpetuating the memory of the Eighth Air Force. Two Society/Foundation Board Members, John Greenwood and Bob Vickers, led the way from this quarter in supporting the American Air Museum over the years (and both also became active members of the American Air Museum Board). Since the 8AFMMF Board considered Duxford the obvious centre on which to concentrate their representation in Europe, they contributed funds towards restoration projects such as the B-17 Flying Fortress and P-47 Thunderbolt, and memora-

The first significant exhibition relating to United States Second World War air power was the Eighth Air Force Exhibit in the side annex of hangar No 3. Opened by Major General John W Huston, Chief, Office of Air Force History on 17 September 1980, the Exhibit, detailing the history of the 8th Air Force, was in place for 17 years. General Huston was a B-17 navigator flying out of Bury St Edmunds in 1944. Seen here following the opening ceremony he is accompanied by three former Eighth Air Force airmen: George Vanden Heuval (P-51 pilot) extreme left, John Greenwood (B-17 navigator), and extreme right, John Woolnough (B-24 pilot). Greenwood was Chairman of the 8th Air Force Memorial and Museum Foundation and John Woolnough the founder of the 8th Air Force Historical Society, the major veterans organisation.

bilia for a permanent exhibit on the Eighth Air Force in one of Duxford's existing hangars. The word spread about the American collection which attracted more American visitors, including many Second World War veterans.

As the collection grew, it became clear that there was not only scope but a need for something more ambitious than the existing Eighth Air Force exhibition which was then housed in an annex to one of the hangars where the prime American aircraft were on show. However, to establish, preserve and display a representative aircraft collection and house it in a purpose-built hangar would cost a million dollars (£700,000).

In September 1980 the IWM established a corporation known as the United States Army Air Forces Collection with the aim of qualifying for tax exemption on gifts from US citizens.

In 1983 the arrival of a B-52 that eventually became the centrepiece of the Museum was largely to dictate the building's design. Plans developed in favour of a grand scheme, not only embracing the 1942-45 USAAF connection but all American military aviation connections with the UK. To attract donations in the United States on the scale required, any appeal had to be broadened beyond the Eighth and Ninth Air Forces. By adding First World War and Cold War elements the main theme

Children of a 1989 school party picking out wartime US airfields on the indicator board in the Eighth Air Force Exhibit. Housed in the annex of Hangar 3, this was the first permanent exhibition honouring American air force associations with the UK and was partly funded by the 8th Air Force Memorial Museum Foundation. (DXP CN 89-41-8)

would be better seen in its historical context. In short, the project was being transformed into a tribute to US air power.

In June 1986 the US Internal Revenue Services granted the USAAF Collections permanent tax exemption status, identifying it as a public charity. The way was now open for a major fund-raising programme in America. Retired USAF Major General James E McInerney Jr, a Washington DC defence consultant, was brought on board to help put together a Committee. A former RAF Staff College student and distinguished Vietnam combat pilot, Jim McInerney proved then and continues to be a central figure and stalwart supporter of the Museum.

Duxford's American aircraft collection was already by then widely acclaimed to be the most impressive outside the USA and as such justified the expansion and scale of the planned presentation to embrace US combat aircraft from all conflicts world-wide, although the main emphasis would still be those Second World War forces based in Britain. The scheme had grown to such a degree that it was expected to cost up to £15 million with a state of the art building designed by Norman Foster to be known as The American Air Museum in Britain. Fifteen million

pounds was a daunting sum. The Museum hoped to secure just under half in the UK as advice from American contacts suggested $10 million (£7 million) to be the highest realistic target in the USA.

An immediate start was made in recruiting people of influence to serve on the Campaign Board. Senator John Tower, long-time Senator for Texas and Chairman of the extremely influential Senate Armed Services Committee (which played a key role in the arms build up during the Reagan administration) was a known Anglophile and accepted the invitation to become Co-Chairman of the US Appeal Campaign in May 1988. Marshal of the Royal Air Force Sir John Grandy, then Chairman of the Imperial War Museum as well as Constable and Governor of Windsor Castle, was named UK Co-Chairman. Sir John had served as a fighter pilot during the Battle of Britain and went on to become Chief of the Air Staff.

The Campaign involved a large scale fund raising effort aimed at wealthy individuals, foundations and corporations – especially the defence industry. Direct mail approaches were also planned to some 50,000 individuals from mailing lists generously provided without

Sir John Grandy, Joint Chairman of the American Air Museum in Britain Campaign, centre, and Dr Alan Borg, IWM's Director General, show Lady Margaret Thatcher the model of the American Air Museum during her visit to the main museum at 'Lambeth' in 1989. (IWM-42-2)

Senator John G Tower poses in the cockpit of the Old Flying Machine Company's TBM Avenger during a visit to Duxford on 18 June 1990. This aircraft was specially painted in the colours of the personal TBM flown by George Bush while serving with the US Navy during the Second World War. It was hoped that while US President, George Bush might have been able to come to Duxford when visiting the UK, but this was not to be. John Tower also served with the US Navy. He first became a Senator in 1961, later becoming Chairman of the Senate Armed Services Committee and was highly influential in determining US defence policy during the final years of the Cold War period. A great anglophile, John Tower was joint Chairman of the American Air Museum Campaign from 1988 until his untimely death three years later. (DUX 90-11-4)

charge by the 8th Air Force Historical Society, Air Force Association and Confederate Air Force.

In 1989, events at the British Embassy in Washington DC hosted by British Ambassador, Sir Anthony Acland and Sir John Grandy marked the official launch of the Campaign leading to the first major pledges from Boeing and Mr Armand Hammer.

From June 1990, the direct mail campaign got underway whose main signatory was a true Second World War American hero, Lieutenant General James H 'Jimmy' Doolittle. His squadron of B-25s, later to become known as the 'Tokyo Raiders', had carried out attacks on the Japanese mainland from the aircraft carrier USS *Hornet* in 1942. General Doolittle's letter invited prospective donors to become a Founding Member with a contribution of $25 or more. Members would then receive regular updates and incentives to make further donations. During the first year $520,000 came in from some 15,700 donors - a much better response than had been anticipated.

To raise the profile of the Campaign Senator Tower briefed President Bush on the project and sought his permission to paint the Grumman Avenger at Duxford to represent the President's own aircraft from his US Navy service in the Pacific during the Second World War. Royal acknowledgement was obtained when His Royal Highness The Duke of Kent, himself a pilot who had also served in the Army, agreed to become Patron.

In the autumn of 1990 Senator Tower relinquished his Co-Chairmanship owing to other commitments. This was a great loss as John Tower had been an influential member of the Board. Tragically, on 5 April 1991, Senator Tower and one of his daughters were killed in an air accident at Brunswick, Georgia.

January 1991 saw the outbreak of the Gulf War, and fund raising was put on hold for the duration of that conflict. Following the repulse of Iraqi forces, Sir John Grandy met Prince Bandar, Saudi Ambassador to the United States, in May 1991 to brief him on the project. Prince Bandar was keen to help and there were strong indications that a substantial donation from the Kingdom of Saudi Arabia could be on the cards.

Meanwhile, the need for a new US Co-Chairman remained. One of the Board Members, retired Air Force Major General Ramsay D Potts, had been a distinguished bomber pilot during the war, most famously leading one of the Liberator B-24 units on the low-level bomber attacks on the Ploesti oil refineries on 1 August 1943. Ramsay Potts had also been the wartime Group Commander of James Stewart, the Hollywood actor, former Eighth Air Force B-24 pilot and American Air Museum Founding Member. At the suggestion of Ramsay Potts,

Jimmy Stewart approached fellow movie star Charlton Heston to take over the role of US Co-Chairman. Mr Heston had been a wartime radio gunner flying in B-25 Mitchells with a squadron in the Aleutian Islands. He gracefully accepted the post in June that year and his involvement brought a much needed famous name to the head of the US fund-raising. Soon afterwards came confirmation of the Saudi donation of a million dollars. This was a huge coup and enabled detailed design to proceed, bringing realisation of the project closer.

In 1992 Jimmy Stewart was guest of honour at a dinner in Beverly Hills in the presence of HRH The Duke of Kent. The Campaign was going extremely well with what had become a series of high profile celebrity events in the US which helped to spread the word, attract important media attention and would often bring the bonus of further significant donations.

Then, in December 1992, the Campaign suffered a great blow when Sir John Grandy, a leading light from the start and highly instrumental in the success of the fund raising Campaign to date, became ill and was unable to continue as UK Co-Chairman. Fortunately, successor to Sir John in the role of Chairman of the Imperial War Museum, Field Marshal The Lord Bramall (who was also Her Majesty's Lord Lieutenant for London) quickly stepped into the role. Lord Bramall had served in the D-Day landings and right through North/West Europe up to the German surrender. He had risen to Chief of the Defence Staff, notably during the Falklands conflict. Like Sir John, Lord Bramall proved to be a dedicated leader and key player in seeing the project through to fruition.

Outline planning permission for the building was obtained early in 1993, but work could not begin until a sizeable amount of the target figure, then £7.5 million, was secured. Fund raising in the UK now began in earnest with a reception at St James's Palace, London in June 1993. This was an auspicious event with several hundred guests, including many well known British and American personalities, who were addressed by Patron HRH The Duke of Kent, Lord Bramall and Charlton Heston. Mrs Michael Heseltine, wife of the Deputy Prime Minister and Imperial War Museum Trustee, came on board as Chairman of the UK Appeal Committee.

Charlton Heston, famous for such movie epics as *Ben Hur*, poses with the B-25 Mitchell during a visit to Duxford on 21 June 1992. During the Second World War Charlton Heston served as an air gunner on B-25 Mitchells of the 28th Bomb Group operating from the Aleutian Islands. (DX CN 92-8-7)

HRH Duke of Kent talks with Colonel Robert Morgan and his wife at Duxford, 14 May 1993. Bob Morgan was the crew captain of the famous *Memphis Belle*, now the only surviving B-17F that took part in the early operations of Eighth Air Force heavy bombers and subject of an excellent William Wyler wartime documentary. (DUX 93-11-12)

Georgia Frontiere, a Co-Chairman of the US Campaign, shares a joke with veteran comedian Bob Hope at the Los Angeles event, 7 April 1994. A foremost supporter of the American Air Museum in Britain, Georgia Frontiere is well known in the United States for her top football team the 'Rams'. (Berliner 41587-21)

Three stalwarts of the US Campaign Board in conversation at the Los Angles dinner. Major General's William Lyon and James E McInerney and Marshall P Cloyd. General Lyon served with the 6th Ferrying Group during the Second World War and was involved in evacuation and ferrying flights during the Korean War. General McInerney was a Cold War era fighter pilot who flew combat in Vietnam and had over 5000 flying hours to his credit when he retired in 1980. Marshall Cloyd, president of an international freight contract firm, served with the US Navy. His father was an Eighth Air Force HQ officer in Britain. (Berliner 41589-1)

HRH The Duke of York talks with 90 year-old John Leland Atwood at the Los Angeles dinner in April 1994. Lee Atwood, a former head of North American Aviation, was one of the design team that produced the famous Mustang and he was later involved in the development of the Sabre and Super Sabre jet fighters. (Berliner 41595-26)

HRH The Duke of York talks with H Ross Perot Junior and his wife during the Los Angles event. Son of the US Reform Party founder and prominent contender for the White House in 1992, Ross Perot Junior is a distinguish pilot. In 1982 he set a speed record for a round the world flight in a helicopter with J W Coburn. Their Bell 206C, named Sprit of Texas, flew around the circumference of the earth in 29 days, 3 hours and 8 minutes, starting and ending at Fort Worth. (Berliner 41588-19)

Activities in the USA continued apace and His Royal Highness The Duke of York, who had served as a naval helicopter pilot from the HMS *Invincible* during the Falklands War, was present at a series of events in 1994 including a dinner hosted by two Campaign Board members, retired USAF Major General William Lyon, a combat pilot in Korea who later became Chief of the Air Force Reserve (1975-79), then with significant property and airline businesses in California. His joint host was Mrs Georgia Frontiere, owner of the highly successful American football team the 'Rams'. Mrs Frontiere, a trained singer, had sung for troops returning from the war and often sang at American Air Museum events including a glamorous concert which she staged entitled 'Stars Who Served'.

Another great celebrity who had entertained troops at Duxford during the war, Bob Hope, was guest of honour at a dinner at Beverly Hills. In typical style, he amused the audience by announcing his intention to return to Duxford to search for something he had lost under one of the aircraft seats. Founding Members were thanked for their support by Charlton Heston at a reception the following evening in the Santa Monica Museum of Flying. During his stay Prince Andrew briefed Walter Annenberg on the project, resulting in a pledge of $200,000 from the Annenberg Foundation.

In 1994 the huge success of the direct mail campaign was under threat following the death of the main signatory, General Doolittle at the grand age of 96. Help was quickly at hand when the General's son, Colonel John Doolittle, who had flown B-26 Marauders in North Africa during the war, took over his late father's role and the mailings were soon back on course. The following year was crucial with all the attendant publicity for the fiftieth anniversary of the end of the Second World War; sympathies for the American Air Museum in Britain project would never be stronger.

Ex-Prime Minister Baroness Thatcher proved an extremely popular guest of honour at a fund-raising dinner in Houston, Texas in February 1995. The Houston contingent of the American Air Museum Board, Marshall P Cloyd, Ben F Love and Philip J Carroll, were key players in this, one of the most successful of all the Museum's events. Mr Cloyd's father had served in the Eighth and Ben Love had been a B-17 pilot. Mr Carroll was Executive Vice President (Administration) of the Shell Oil Company, and encouraged support both from his own and other corporations for the project. Shortly after the Houston dinner, the USA Campaign had raised around £1.7 million ($2.5 million).

Prince Andrew enjoys a joke with Walker Mahurin. Fighter ace 'Bud' Mahurin flew Thunderbolts with the Eighth Air Force in England, and during the Korean War was shot down in a Sabre and taken prisoner. (Berliner 41585-6)

Up to this time the Imperial War Museum, which was Government funded, had been required to raise considerable funds towards capital projects in order to trigger any additional Government grant. The implementation of the National Lottery by Prime Minister John Major's Government, including the availability of funds for museum capital projects from the Heritage Lottery Fund, brought an air of optimism. This was well founded, for Lottery funds would prove to be the key to the project finally going ahead.

In these early days of the National Lottery there were substantial funds to be distributed but few projects 'ready to go'. This situation worked favourably for the American Air Museum which had all planning permis-sions and required only the balance of funds to allow the project to proceed. Mindful that the Lottery was British money for British causes, the Museum's application for £6.5 million emphasised the fact that the provision of hangar space for this fine collection of American combat aircraft would free up covered space for important examples of rare British aircraft. Following submission of the

Ted Inman being interviewed by a television crew on 1 August 1985 about the announcement of the Lottery grant. Duxford's B-17G *Mary Alice* in the background. (DXP CN 95-32-23)

Museum's application, there followed some tense weeks for everyone who had worked so hard to make the American Air Museum in Britain a reality. Then, on 25 July 1995, official notification was given that the full £6.5 million requested had been granted. The Heritage Lottery Fund Trustees had recognised that the overwhelming American military presence in East Anglia during the Second World War and its impact on our culture should legitimately be considered part of the UK's national heritage. Doubt was banished: the American Air Museum would be built.

There was now great activity to get construction underway as soon as possible with a ground breaking ceremony in September to capitalise on the current transatlantic 'fiftieth anniversary mood'. A US veteran, Major James 'Jim' Stokes, who had served at Duxford as a P-47 Thunderbolt pilot with the 78th Fighter Group, carried out the official ground breaking. Of more than 500 guests, 300 were USAAF veterans. Speakers included the US Ambassador, Admiral William Crowe, Colonel John Doolittle, Lord Bramall and Mrs Heseltine.

The fact that the American Air Museum in Britain building was underway, plus the major part of the finance having been secured, stimulated interest and brought several large donations from both sides of the Atlantic, including a bequest of $100,000 from Ruth Eaker, widow of Ira Eaker, the pioneering Eighth Air Force Commanding General.

The direct mail campaign went from strength to strength, generating in excess of $200,000 with over 8,000 new Founding Members in 1995, and in the autumn of 1996 the membership stood at 55,000. By January 1997 the deficit was under a million pounds. Promotional events continued to be successful, helped by celebrity guests of honour, notably HRH The Duke of York who had become an enthusiastic supporter, Lloyd Bentsen (former US Treasury Secretary) and Tom Landry (former coach of the Dallas Cowboys). Both Mr Bentsen and Mr Landry had served as Second World War bomber pilots.

With the Museum building nearing completion, Lord Bramall invited Her Majesty The Queen to conduct the Opening Ceremony on 1 August 1997, and the invitation was accepted. The high level publicity generated undoubtedly provided an extra incentive for Founding Members, other individuals and corporations to contribute.

Air shows apart, the opening ceremony was the biggest event ever organised by the Imperial War Museum and was a huge celebration of Anglo-American co-operation held in the 50th anniversary year of the establishment of the United States Air Force. Her Majesty The Queen was joined by HRH The Prince Philip, HRH The Duke of Kent and HRH The Duke of York, making this a major Royal occasion. Secretary of the United States Air Force Dr Sheila Widnall was senior US Representative. Flypasts by Duxford based aircraft, the B-17 Flying Fortress, P-47 Thunderbolt and two P-51 Mustangs, followed by four USAF F-15s from nearby RAF Lakenheath, gave tribute to those who served and many of whom gave their lives, to put the seal on this memorable day.

Soon after the opening of the Museum the sum raised in gifts and pledges stood at over £11 million with total costs of £11,193,000. The continuing strong performance of the direct mail campaign dictated that this part of the Campaign should be continued to provide a fund for the provision of further exhibits. There were also further enhancements planned for the building itself such as a shop, café and Founding Members Room - an exclusive facility for members visiting the Museum.

The membership was expected to decline over a period of time, but prospecting for new members brought new interest; donors joining after the Museum's opening were known as Sustaining Members. In 1999 direct mail brought in $1.3 million, making this the most successful of its kind in museum appeals. The on-going fund proffers well for the future of the Museum with plans for its extension now in hand.

What at the outset appeared a formidable objective proved to be an outstanding success, thanks to the considerable generosity of some 70,000 Founding and Sustaining Members, other individuals and corporate donors, the persistence and energy of the staff and Trustees of the Imperial War Museum plus those supporters in Britain with volunteers in America who had given so much to make the Museum a reality.

THE BUILDING

There are people who dislike Norman Foster buildings and there are those that adore them, but no one can be indifferent to the work of this brilliant innovative architect. His designs for the Shanghai Bank in Hong Kong and the Stansted Airport terminal brought him recognition as a leader in his profession. He first visited Duxford in 1985 with two Cambridge friends who were not pleased with the shape of a new hangar about to be built close to the M11. Norman Foster offered to design a more aesthetic building but it was too late to make changes.

Impressed by Norman Foster's ideas and learning that he had an interest in historic aviation, in April 1986 Edward Inman proposed to the Trustees' that the architect be approached about designing a special hangar to hold the collection of American aircraft. In the event Norman Foster's enthusiasm was such that he offered to waive his fees for preparing some initial proposals. The Trustees of the USAAF Collection had previously decided that to further interest with their fund-raising campaign the hangar building should be of an inspirational design, so Norman Foster's positive interest was welcomed.

In respect of planning and design issues, while the building must be large enough to hold the 20 aircraft selected, it also had to be of a restrained appearance appropriate to the rural location. The architect's concept was soon forthcoming and featured an elliptical shaped building. His reasoning followed that in controlling costs the design should be simple and not compete visually with the aircraft exhibits therein. To that end the architectural form would be developed from the aircraft that needed to be housed, notably the B-52 Stratofortress which required the roof span to be at least 90 metres to cover this and the other 20 aircraft in the collection. To further control costs some of the aircraft should be suspended from the roof constructed by a technique not unlike the stressed skin structure employed in aircraft. A vertical glass wall on the amputated end of this finger-tip shape would provide the main natural lighting. To achieve a dramatic visual experience, the visitor entrance was to be at a raised level confronting the nose of the B-52 and providing a panorama of the whole collection. Perimeter ramp walkways on both inner sides of the building allowed visitors to move down to ground level for close inspection of the exhibits. Room for ancillary exhibitions, retail space and plant area would be in the 'nose' of the building around and below the raised entrance level.

An exciting concept it met with the Trustees unanimous approval. Models of the building were made by the architects for display purposes, notably to use at fund-raising events. Foster Associates worked with Ove Arup and Partners, structural engineers, on the outline designs and by early spring 1987 Belfield & Everest,

quantity surveyors, were brought in to do costing. At this stage all three were working on a fees on account basis. In the event the figure arrived at was £10 million which with the proposed Imax cinema, all interior fitting-out and three years inflation allowance totalled a daunting £15 million. With only limited funds in hand further design work was restricted during the following two years until the financial situation looked more promising.

Planning permission was applied for in January 1990, by which time the structural engineers had refined the roof structure. This, plus the decision to eliminate the Imax cinema and postpone retail fixtures, reduced the estimated building cost from £10 million to £8 million.

James E Stokes, wearing part of his Second World War uniform, cuts the ceremonial first turf on 8 September 1995. Jim Stokes flew P-47 Thunderbolts from Duxford with the 83rd Fighter Squadron from June 1943 until February 1944. (DUX 95-13-32)

The architectural team could no longer be expected to continue on deferred fees so in the spring of 1991 a sum was made available by the IWM to forward design work. It was hoped that this would lead to more refinements and budget savings. Further to this end suppliers of steel, glass and other materials were approached for free or reduced cost supplies with, generally, favourable receptions.

With the pledge of $1 million from the Saudis and the receipt of planning permission in August 1991 the architects and their associates were asked to commence detailed design. Further refinements established the building costs at £7.5 million, a substantial reduction over the original estimate. Design work was completed by early 1993 and a start on construction then awaited sufficient funds. In fact, at this stage it was obvious that the future of the whole project was dependent upon a successful bid for a Heritage Lottery grant. With favourable reports in this direction and the necessity to keep up the momentum of the fund-raising campaign and associated morale, tenders were invited in July 1995 prior to the actual public announcement of the lottery grant. Of the five companies approached the contract was awarded to J Sisk & Son Ltd, chiefly due to the firm's good attitude.

The schedule called for work to commence in September and to take 16 months: precisely, 29 September 1995 to 29 January 1997. The main structure had to be far enough advanced by August the following year to allow the aircraft to be installed before the glass front was erected. After the symbolic ground breaking ceremony on 8 September, the contractor's machinery appeared on site, and on the appointed day work began.

Ground work underway, 16 October 1995. Excavations down to three metres resulted in 10,000 cubic metres of the chalk and soil. Deposited at the south corner of the site it was later used as backfill. (DXP 95-41-77)

Dr. Alan Borg, Robert Crawford and architect Sir Norman Foster watching the flying display following the ground breaking ceremony on 8 September 1995. The 500 guests included 300 US veterans. (DUX 95-13-97)

The first task was excavations to three metres deep with the resulting 10,000 cubic metres of spoil being dispersed in the south-west corner of the airfield, an area below the level of the runway. Excavated material was also piled behind the revetment near the public road for use as back fill to the new building. Thanks to favourable autumn weather the ground work was completed in November. The next stage involved steel reinforced foundations, followed by construction of the retaining walls for roof support. The roof, by far the biggest single element of the building, was begun in February 1996, but work on the pre-cast concrete panels, which were made off-site by sub-contractor R J O'Rourke Civil Construction, was subject to delays. Steel arms to secure the roof to the rest of the structure were also delivered late. These delays, amounting to three or four weeks, appeared to blight the construction schedule and necessitated Sisk's revising the programme in order to make up time.

As Ove Arup works manager, Vernon Price, commented: 'Mathematically the building is the simplest in the world to understand but in terms of its construction it is probably one of the most complex'. The intricate shape of the roof is best rationalised by following the geometry of a torus – that of a doughnut. The curving surface of the roof is generated by two radii of 278 metres and 64 metres. In this way all the elements of the roof have the same curvature, simplifying the construction process by enabling the re-use of underprop formwork which in turn provided both economy and efficiency. The structural support of the roof is equally ingenious. The transfer of forces from the concrete roof to the base structure is achieved by casting a steel section into the edge of the roof, connected to steel arms which then transmit the loads through small, moving 'pinpoint' connections to the base. Similar in principle to bridge bearings, these pinpoint connections allow for any thermal expansion or contraction of the roof canopy. At its widest point at the front of the building, a 90 metre span, the roof canopy is solidly fixed to the base structure. At the rear of the building the separation between roof and base structure is greatest, providing maximum tolerance in free movement.

Said to be the largest pre-cast concrete structure in Europe, the roof was completed by mid-summer 1996. The steel supports removed, the ceremonial Topping Out was performed on 19 July; in this case the presentation of a silver trowel by the contractors to the Director of Duxford Airfield, Edward Inman. However, the three week lag had yet to be made up and the first aircraft could not be brought in until the floor was completed. Moreover, efforts to resolve the delay problems elevated building cost by 4.4%.

Entrances in the glass wall being of limited size, complete aircraft had to be installed in the building before

Steel reinforcing of the sub-structure placed ready for concrete pouring to begin. A 40 grade concrete was employed on most of the substructure. (DXP 95-41-73)

Work on retaining walls and columns, 7 December 1995. Fortunately, the winter was not severe and progress was not hampered unduly by weather. (DXP CN 95-41-261)

Roof construction commenced in February 1996, a light sprinkling of snow had fallen when this photograph was taken on the 20th. Loads from the roof are transferred to the abutment structure by way of an upper and lower ring beam, which is spanned by 14 steel arms supporting the whole structure. (DXP CN 96-1-194)

the erection of the glazing. The first aircraft placements, those that had to be suspended from the roof, began on 2 September, a week later than planned. The B-52 and other large aircraft followed and the immediate programme was completed on 16 September, within the time scale allowed for the contract. Later additions had to be taken into the building in sections and reassembled inside. The immediate need was temporary weather protection until the glass front was installed, and to this end plastic sheeting was hung on scaffolding. The erection of the glass front, which has anti-ultra violet properties, was begun by the Italian sub-contractors later that month with completion of this difficult task in December.

By the end of 1996 considerable internal work still had to be carried out including the main lighting and service equipment, including the dehumidification plant. The last facility was to provide the desired environment for the aircraft, a dry, stable atmosphere of 45-55% relative humidity. Two coats of paint on the floor, safety rails to the walk-way ramps and other fixtures and finishes had be carried out, all of which meant that the building contract would not be finished by the contract date of 27 January 1997. This led to the museum staff having to execute their work on the aircraft and other exhibition features while the contractors were still in the building, leading to many frustrations, not least dirt and dust. Indeed, the contractors were still present almost to the date of the official opening. Pre-cast copings were not fixed to the top of the vertical entrance walls until June.

Externally the surrounding ground had to be cleared of building detritus, restored, graded, re-seeded and a boundary fence erected. Painting and several minor finishing works were still in hand in July, plus the considerable task of cleaning the huge front wall and the other glazing which was only completed two days before the official opening by the Queen. That everything was ready in time for 1 August resulted from an intensive workload for both contractors and museum staff during the preceding month.

This seminal design soon won several awards. First, the High Commendation in the British Construction Industry Awards for 1997, then the architects received the Royal Institute of British Architect's premier award, the Stirling Prize in November 1998. The building also won The People's Choice award as a result of an RIBA voting competition. The British Guild of Travel Writers awarded the American Air Museum in Britain their Silver Unicorn trophy for the Tourism Attraction of the Year Award in 1997, and was it was adjudged joint winner in the Royal Fine Arts/ Sky Broadcasting award for Building of the Year.

The accolades aside, such an unusual design brought early operational problems. An unpleasantness was heat in summer months which took air conditioning equipment to rectify. The shape of the building gave poor acoustics and an improved public address system was required. Minor defects became evident, notably a roof leak that was not easily cured. But overall, the building met the requirements admirably, both functionally and aesthetically. Magnificent to behold at close quarters it is also remarkably unobtrusive in the rural landscape, the concrete roof often visually merging with the sky.

Top left: About 800 tons of temporary steel uprights were erected to support the roof. Some 600 jacks were employed and their removal entailed painstaking work to ensure no one roof section was subject to overload. This involved twenty separate 5 mm steps across each of the 600 jacks and took best part of a week. (DUX 96-1-526)

Centre left: Wrapped upper sections of pre-cast roof, size 2.7m by 5m, which sub-contractor Malling Precast made off site. (DUX 96-1-522)

Bottom left: Concreting in situ on a special area of the exterior. The workmen have safety harness. (DUX 96-1-548)

Top right: Roof complete and scaffolding removed. Total weight of the roof is in excess of 6,000 tons. A grey Sarnafil roofing membrane covers the whole exterior. (DUX 96-1-667)

Centre right: Construction of the internal ramps in the mezzanine area. (DUX 96-1-696)

Bottom right: Much like a giant finger tip, the completed building ready for the IWM's American collection. With a view to making this truly comprehensive, in June 1991 the IWM Department of Exhibits and Firearms made a request to the USAF Museum for a P-38, P-40, B-24, AT-6, F-86, F-4, F-5, F-15, F-16, F-18, F-111, A-10, C-130 and U-2. Seven of these types were still being sought when the American Air Museum in Britain was officially opened in August 1997. (DUX 97-53-19)

CONSERVATION

Since the earliest days Imperial War Museum Duxford has had an on-going programme of conserving the aircraft acquired. Few machines deteriorate more rapidly than aircraft when exposed to the humid climate of the British Isles and many of the museum's acquisitions were received in a corroded or damaged state.

Work to repair and preserve requires specialist capability and Duxford has a team of engineers employed full time on such necessary tasks. As the work in hand is frequently far greater than the regular force can manage over even an extended period, skilled volunteers are also employed on a part time basis. All of these are members of the Duxford Aviation Society, an enthusiast group supporting the Imperial War Museum mission.

The first American aircraft received at Duxford was a P-51D Mustang, built up from boxed sections that had lain for many months at the rear of the main building in Lambeth. A B-17G obtained from France was the second and took much time and effort in returning it to a wartime configuration. Both types were to be representative of the US Eighth Air Force, the subject of the original interest in holding a collection of American warplanes. Following a decision to broaden the scope to include not only aircraft from other Second World War combat zones but those of earlier and later conflicts, the number of new acquisitions increased and by the mid-1980s amounted to a score of types which would qualify for inclusion in the American Air Museum.

As the project became more of a reality, conservation planning was dominated by preparation of the aircraft destined for the building. By 1991 ten types had been identified as requiring some degree of work to bring them to the standard required. This standard extended beyond just refurbishing the structure of the aircraft, and included as much of the systems and internal equipment as possible to make them true representations of their operational form. The giant B-52 Stratofortress was in need of major anti-corrosion work, mostly external, and repainting; the B-29 Superfortress, major structural restoration; the B-25 Mitchell, which had been under restoration for some time required another two years to

Many of the aircraft rescued for Duxford have been found stripped of instrumentation. A good example is the engineer's panel of the B-29 Superfortress, here shown in the condition as first found at China Lake and after refurbishment for the flight to the UK. (HU 37466 & HU37378)

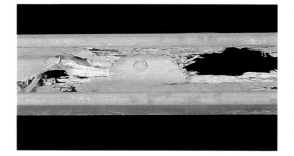

Metal corrosion was the major problem with discarded aircraft that had been exposed to the elements for a considerable time. This is typical of the decay found in many places in the B-29, which externally appeared little harmed during its long years in the China Lake sage brush. (DXP CN 94-56-1)

complete; the C-47 Skytrain, needed refurbishment and repainting; the P-47 Thunderbolt had its restoration delayed due to lack of major structural components; the T-33 jet trainer required an estimated three years restoration work; an F-100 Super Sabre needed a year to restore; TBM-3 Avenger, a further two years on restoration; Stearman PT-17 biplane, complete restoration, and F-4 Phantom II, demodification to 1972 Vietnam standard plus a repaint. Although uncertainty then existed as to whether or not the American Air Museum would be built, it was clear that with other conservation commitments it was unlikely this workload could be completed with current resources. Chris Chippington, Head of Conservation, had a staff of eight officers with engineering skills, two of whom were primarily engaged on vehicle work. These two were diverted to painting aircraft and providing extra engineering assistance, but more engineering input had to be found. One line of assistance secured at this time was an agreement with FFV Aerotech Ltd at Stansted Airport. This aircraft maintenance firm sought projects on which their apprentices could develop skills. Ten apprentices, two or three at a time, with a supervisor undertook work on the B-29 from the summer of 1991, and later the B-25. Nevertheless it was necessary to increase the work force and over the next two years the full-time staff was raised to 13. Additionally, four temporary conservation officers were recruited on 18 month

contracts boosting the total workforce to 17. Recruitment and retaining people skilled in aviation engineering had always been difficult due to the attraction of the high salaries paid by commercial firms, notably at nearby Stansted airport. Although American aircraft continued to have priority other requirements could not be neglected, resulting in little progress with some restorations during the next two years.

In 1995 with word of the successful Lottery bid and a tentative plan to open the American Air Museum building in autumn 1997, there was a necessary urgency to complete conservation requirements on the aircraft in hand earmarked for housing. The building schedule required that the majority of these exhibits were ready for installation during August/ September 1996 before the glass wall was erected. With a renewed need for more skilled men, three temporary members of staff were recruited. To supplement the 'in house' work on the aircraft some restorations were put out to private companies. Because of the Stearman PT-17's poor condition it was at first not considered worthy of rebuilding, but was

A colossal task. Blasting clean the old paintwork of the B-52 using a 'plastic shot' process developed by ICI. The tiny plastic grains are harder than the paint, softer than the metal. (DXP 95-31-4)

taken in hand by Eastern Stearman Ltd of Swanton Morley, Norfolk, which, as their name suggests, were specialists in work on this popular biplane. A Spad replica, the sole First World War representative was also the subject of a contract for preparation by the same firm. A deal with Planes of Fame Museum at Chino, USA involved a restored Meteor being exchanged for an F-86 Sabre. The AT-6 wanted for exhibition was acquired and prepared for the IWM by the Aircraft Restoration Company located at Duxford.

In total 17 aircraft and four vehicles had to be ready for the installation deadline date of 23 August 1996. Eight of these had to be suspended from the roof: T-33, F-100, AT-6, Stearman, Spad, TG-3 glider, Avenger and U-2. Concentrated work by staff assisted by volunteers, about a 50-50 split, over the next twelve months ensured all 'in house' subjects were ready. Most significant in this activity, in terms of magnitude, was the repair and repainting of the B-52 and B-29. An extraordinary engineering effort was put in on the P-47 where wings and tail surfaces had still to be rebuilt and joined to the fuselage at the time of the Lottery award. Unfortunately, the restorations of the Stearman and the Spad were not completed on time, but as these were both reasonably small and relatively lightweight, being of wood/fabric construction, they were lifted up later.

In planning the exhibit display within the new building a decision had been taken at an early date to allow visitors close contact with the aircraft. This was in part dictated by the compact nature of the aircraft display but also by the desire to dispel the remoteness that pervades 'roped off' and enclosed museum exhibits. Propellers and other projections which could cause injury had to be protected, but the aircraft were probably more at risk to damage than any visitors to injury. Not least of concerns for any museum staff are the souvenir collectors who have no respect for exhibits.

The suspension equipment for the aircraft was particularly demanding. The design element was carried out by Norman Harry, OBE, an aeronautical and stress engineer, with approval of suspension fittings design given by DRA Farnborough. The Royal Engineers gave a favourable response to an approach for their assistance to do the actual operation of lifting the aircraft into the roof, only to call off due to other commitments. Instead the installation task was carried out under contract by Vanguard Engineering of Greenford, a company normally engaged in the world-wide installation of heavy

To give the B-52 a complete respray it was necessary to erect scaffolding around it in Hangar 1. (DXP 95-31-43)

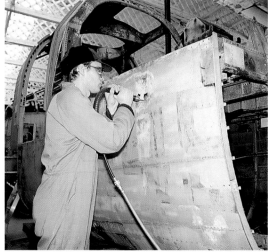

Geoff Cowins spraying demarcation lines on the B-52's tail.
(DXP 95-47-8)

The Duxford Aviation Society aided much of the conservation
work. Two member, Vic Lawson, left, and Norman Osborne, fix a
problem on the nose undercarriage leg of the F-4 Phantom.
(DXP CN 95-19-8)

One of the most remarkable transformations carried out by
Conservation engineers involved turning two battered sections
of B-24 Liberator nose into one excellent exhibit. Here Andy
Robinson drills out rivets so that corroded skin can be replaced.
(DUX 96-99-5)

precision machinery for industry. The roof geometry and planned aircraft attitudes, combined with the need to keep the load distribution on the building within acceptable limits, resulted in the suspension cable angles being far from uniform. This in turn meant that cable loads were not evenly distributed, with those at some aircraft attachment points likely to be very high. Consequently hurried work on designing and manufacturing substantial fittings took place, taking into consideration stress factors and any airframe weakening through concealed modifications incorporating suspension attachments. Delays in construction of the building prevented the conservation task force from commencing installation of the aircraft until a week after the scheduled date. Of the six aircraft that could be suspended the AT-6 gave the

Missing components often had to be manufactured, as in the case of the B-25 tail gun position. The 'Point Fifty' calibre guns being installed by Martin Barnes were a combination of the real and the fabricated. (DUX 96-18-5)

most difficulty. It had been planned to position this in a climbing attitude but this produced unacceptable airframe loading. To overcome the problem its position was revised to straight-and-level 'flight'. Vanguard planned to use a flat-bed hydraulic platform for lifting but this proved untenable because of the different stances of the aircraft. The work was finally done with a 50-ton boom truck, two small cranes plus a variety of winches and chain tackle. When the Stearman and Spad eventually arrived on site it was found that the contractor for the former had not been in a position to design and manufacture suspension point equipment, while those made for the Spad failed under test. Both machines were stored in the new building until the necessary fixtures had been made.

As soon as the initial suspension work was completed the B-52 was wheeled in and then the other types. It was at this juncture that the Building Regulation inspectors insisted on clear corridors across the floor slab for emergency fire exit, thus causing some repositioning of aircraft from the original plan. As there was still on going

contractors' work in the building, chiefly finishers, the conservation staff were further hampered by dirt and dust necessitating protective plastic sheeting over most exhibits. This in addition to the temporary scaffolding and plastic screening hung on 20 September to block the front wall opening following the completion of aircraft installation. An unforeseen and very expensive expedient was made necessary by high winds that began to cause some oscillation of the Avenger. The UH-1 Huey helicopter and the F-86 Sabre, not arriving until after the glass wall was erected, had to be taken into the museum building through the doorway and assembled inside. It was necessary to jack up the B-25 in order to obtain enough height to move the Huey underneath to reach its planned display position. One of the most troubling tasks was installing the replica P-51 Mustang on its pillar. The largely plastic structure first had to be strengthened internally and tested. With restricted space in the area of the building where it was positioned, roof anchor points had to be used to lift the Mustang into position. The work was further complicated by the replica's adverse centre of gravity.

Once all aircraft exhibits were within the new building much work still had to be carried out in situ. In fact, minor tasks continued right up to the opening day. In view of tremendous work-load and the very short time period in which it had to be completed, the conservation staff, permanent and temporary, plus DAS volunteers, accomplished an extraordinary feat.

Freedom of public access to the exhibits has undoubtedly proved a success, although pilfering and slight damage does occur. During the first two years of the American Air Museum's opening a number of small items were taken from aircraft, including tyre and oleo dust caps, armament pins, servicing labels, electric fuses and static discharge aerials. Damage was mainly scratching of paintwork and glazing, the B-29 suffering most, while the B-25 and Huey gathered some graffiti. Youngsters were the major offenders, frequently opening panels and turning propellers when staff were absent. Of more concern was a boy walking on the wing of the C-47 and the finding of footprints on top of the Huey!

Above: Push! DAS member Jim Morgan aids the entry of the F-86 Sabre into the American Air Museum building. (DUX 97-1-494)

Opposite page:

Top: IWM Conservation officers Martin Barnes (left) and Keith Trigg work on B-24M Liberator in Hangar 5. The name and motif were adornments gained some years earlier at Lackland AFB when the aircraft was painted up to represent a B-24 of the 93rd Bomb Group. (DX 99-97-22)

Centre left: First aircraft to be suspended from the roof was the U-2 which Vanguard Engineering's rigging crew secured. Advice on suspension was obtained from a Norwegian air museum which has the only example of a U-2 in Europe. The giant B-52 can be seen in the photograph standing outside the building ready for entry. (Time lapse 4/9/96-4)

Bottom left: The F-100 Super Sabre at 5 tons was the heaviest aircraft suspended, the degree of pitch and roll angles required having to be set at ground level before lifting. The most critical part was the transfer of weight from the cranes to the suspension cables, the latter all having to pick up at precisely the same instant to avoid overload at any one point and possible damage to the aircraft. (Time lapse 7/9/96-29)

Bottom right: The replica Spad was the last aircraft to be suspended, made particularly difficult as most of the floor based aircraft were then in the building,. The tricky task was performed by four winch operators on crane booms. All eight suspensions were achieved without any damage to the aircraft involved. (DUX CN 97-1-107)

THE COLLECTION – The Aircraft Exhibits

The individual types now on display in the American Air Museum in Britain are here presented in the order that they were acquired by the IWM.

Duncan Cubitt – FlyPast Magazine

North American P-51D Mustang

The major feature of the American Air Museum is the collection of aircraft used by United States military and naval services during the Twentieth Century. Aircraft from the First and Second World Wars are now rare, albeit that following the conclusion of those conflicts they were plentiful but, as so often happens, at the time they were not seen to be of historic interest. Thus, when the IWM began to build its American collection for static display in the 1970s, many representative types were no longer readily available. Moreover, many remaining examples were in very poor condition, requiring major restoration work. While the IWM now has its own team of engineers to attend to this, much assistance is and has been forthcoming from volunteers, principally the Duxford Aviation Society (DAS) One of the most successful aircraft of the Second World War, the Mustang through

its range and performance, played the major part in establishing and maintaining air superiority in enemy airspace, particularly over Europe. Originally designed in 1940 for the RAF, the fighter was powered by a low-altitude rated Allison engine. Found wanting as a defensive fighter it was used for fast tactical reconnaissance duties in support of ground forces. The USAAF showed little interest in the type until a later model was fitted with the Packard-built version of the Rolls-Royce Merlin 60 series engine which had a two-stage supercharger. With performance that equalled or bettered the enemy opposition, apart from in rate of climb, the P-51B Mustang and subsequent models provided the long-range fighter the USAAF urgently needed to sustain its daylight bomber operations. The Mustang had internal fuel capacity that gave a radius of action of some 350 miles from home base, and carrying jettisonable fuel tanks under the wings it could fly anywhere the bombers went. By the end of hostilities the USAAF had some 2,300 P-51s in 60 fighter squadrons operating in Europe. The Eighth Air Force had 42 squadrons, the Fifteenth 12 and six served with the

Lieutenant Frank E Oiler, pilot, and his ground crew chief with the real *Sherman Was Right!* While flown by another member of the 84th Fighter Squadron this Mustang was shot down by ground fire on 4th March 1945.

Ninth. There were also a dozen USAAF squadrons using P-51s for tactical reconnaissance. The RAF and Commonwealth air forces had 20 Mustang, equipped squadrons at this time. The P-51 was also used by several USAAF squadrons in the war with Japan and later by the USAF in Korea. More than 10,500 Mustangs and variants were produced.

In 1967 the IWM was given a late production P-51D as a gift from the people of Canada. Following two years service with the USAAF it had been transferred to the RCAF in 1947 and served with Nos 402 and 420 Squadrons before retirement. Becoming a 'gate guardian' at RCAF St Jean, Quebec, it reposed on a pedestal for some twelve years. Removed, dissembled and packed in nine crates, the Mustang arrived at Gatwick on 17/18 December 1968 and reached the IWM early in the new year. There it remained crated at the Lambeth site for three years, there being no room for display until refurbishment of the main building. When Duxford came under IWM control this Mustang, RCAF serial 9246 , USAAF serial 44-73979, was moved there in December 1971, becoming the first restoration project largely handled by members of the East Anglian Aviation Society, an enthusiasts organisation. When assembled the aircraft was painted to represent the P-51D flown by the last wartime CO of the 78th Fighter Group at Duxford, Colonel John Landers. *Big Beautiful Doll* was an eye-catching attraction at Duxford for a number of years, but after a major overhaul the aircraft was taken to the London building and suspended over the main gallery.

When an American Air Museum was projected at Duxford, it was expected that the Mustang would eventually be returned, but on consideration of the expense involved and the need to maintain some recognition of US air power at Lambeth it was decided that another

Above: When the main museum at Southwark was refurbished there was a need to give some representation to the USAAF. The only suitable aircraft then available was the Mustang and this was transferred from Duxford and suspended in the main hall. *Big Beautiful Doll* was disassembled into main components and transferred to London by road in 1989.

Bottom left: First of the many. The Imperial War Museum's American warplane collection began with a P-51D Mustang obtained from Canada in 1967. Passed to Duxford it was beautifully restored by Duxford Aviation Society members in co-operation with the Museum and painted in the colours of a wartime American CO of the station's personal aircraft. Colonel John Landers, a fighter ace credited with 9 air and 20 strafing victories, commanded the 78th Fighter Group from February to July 1945. Before his death in 1989 Landers made a return visit to Duxford and saw the Mustang painted in his honour. (HU31030)

Mustang should be found for Duxford. While around a hundred P-51s are known to exist world-wide, most are airworthy and therefore of great value, fetching upward of a million US dollars for private flying. Being unable to find an airframe suitable for static display, in November 1996 the IWM agreed to purchase an accurate fibreglass replica owned by the Old Flying Machine Co at Duxford. The sum paid, £20,000, included a complete overhaul and authentic fitments by the vendors together with a paint scheme representative of a Duxford based 78th Fighter Group Mustang. Made of fibreglass over a steel frame, the bogus Mustang had once adorned a store window in London's Oxford Street.

The replica was painted to represent P-51D serial 44-63209, coded WZ-S of the 84th Fighter Squadron, which carried the slogan *Sherman Was Right!* (a comment

Positioned on its pillar and secured, only an expert would know this was not the real thing. IWM staff members Haron Kinl and Geoff Cousins in the 'cherry picker'. (DUX CN 97-1-668)

on the famous pronouncement of Civil War General Sherman that war 'is all hell'). The real 44-63209, assigned to 1st Lt Frank E Oiler, failed to return with another pilot, Lt Louis Hereford, from an escort mission on 3 March 1945.

Mounted on a 3.5 metre pillar in the museum, the replica is realistic enough to be taken as a genuine aircraft by the uninitiated. In avoiding the radiator scoop the pillar attachment point had to be made some three feet aft of the Mustang's centre of gravity. A counter balance was required which involved conservation officer Geoff Cousins crawling up the rear fuselage to fix iron weights. Unfortunately 110 lb of weights slipped from his hands resulting in a very large repair to the hole through the bottom of the fuselage! Taken into the building in sections during February 1997, the restricted space available at this time presented difficulties with installation. The Mustang had to be lifted vertically on cables before the supporting pillar could be placed underneath.

Crew	One
Engine	One 1,650 hp (1,230 kW) liquid-cooled Packard V-1650-7 Merlin (licence built Rolls-Royce).
Dimensions	Wing span 37 ft (11.89 m). Length 32 ft 3 in (9.85 m).
Weight	7,125 lb (3,232 kg) empty. 11,600 lb (5,262 kg) loaded.
Armament	Six 0.50 in calibre machine guns. Two 1,000 lb bombs in lieu of jettisonable fuel tanks.
Performance	Top speed 437 mph (703 kph) at 25,000 ft (7,620 m). Cruise speed 210-320 mph (338-514 kph). Service ceiling 41,900 ft (12,771 m). Combat range 950 miles (1,528 km) on internal fuel or up to 2,300 miles (3,700 km) with drop tanks.

Boeing B-17G Fortress

Arguably the most famous American warplane of all time, the 1935 B-17 prototype was the world's first all-metal, four-engine, monoplane bomber. A journalist's comment that the new aircraft was a 'flying fortress' led the manufacturer to register that name for the B-17. Only ordered in small numbers due to its cost relative to competing designs, the pre-war B-17 was none the less the vehicle used to develop the US Army Air Corps' doctrine of daylight, high-altitude precision bombing. Redesigned in 1941 to give it heavy defensive armament, the Fortress became the pioneer and backbone of the US

The IWM acquired its Fortress in 1975. The aircraft, USAAF serial 44-83735, is a B-17G-95-DL model built by Douglas at Long Beach, California in April/May 1945 and delivered to the USAAF at Rome Army Air Base, New York on 21 May. The war in Europe being over, there was little service use for B-17s and in November 1945 this aircraft eventually went to the Reclamation Finance Center at Altus Army Air Base where most unwanted warplanes were sold for scrap metal. However, 44-83735 survived the breakers. In the early post-war years there was a demand for transport aircraft by civil airlines which could

Outside a Creil hangar in the 1960s, F-BDRS in its heyday of IGN service. The row of four small windows in the fuselage rear cabin would be one of many civil use items that Duxford engineers later removed.

Eighth Air Force's strategic bombing offensive from Britain. The fierce air battles between unescorted B-17s and the Luftwaffe added credence to the name Flying Fortress and caught the public's imagination. A total of 12,731 Fortresses were produced and by the end of hostilities there were 108 squadrons with the Eighth Air Force in England and 24 with the Fifteenth Air Force in Italy. Fortresses were also used by RAF Bomber and Coastal Commands.

not be met. The good flight stability of the B-17 led to several bombers having all combat equipment removed and being converted for passenger or cargo use. With few flying hours, this aircraft was selected for conversion and for five years was operated by the president of Philippine Airlines, under the US civil registration NL68629 with the name *San Miguel*.

By the early 1950s more purpose-built aircraft for passenger and cargo transport were available and the Fortress was retired. At this time the French Institut Géographique National (IGN) was engaged on an extended programme of photographic mapping of French colonies and dependencies. The B-17 with its high-altitude capability and unpressurised crew accommodation

Cannibalised for engines and nose transparency, F-BDRS sits forlornly on a hardstanding among the trees. The sight that greeted the Duxford recovery team in the summer of 1975. (MH24985)

The interior of the rear fuselage cabin. Comfortable seats and curtains at the windows, a far cry from the spartan wartime bomber interior. (MH24982)

was near ideal for this purpose with the added advantage of being comparatively cheap to buy. N68629 then became registered F-BDRS after purchase by the French on 23 August 1952 and was given the name *Chateau de Verneuil*. Employed on photographic survey work for the best part of twenty years, it was grounded at Creil in 1971 for use as a source of spares for other IGN B-17s. Two years later Euroworld, an aviation trading company run by entrepreneur Ted White, purchased an airworthy B-17 from IGN and the grounded F-BDRS. Through an agreement with the IWM, White was permitted to bring and maintain the airworthy B-17 at Duxford, this aircraft becoming the famous *Sally B*. F-BDRS was offered on loan to the IWM as a static exhibit, a party of DAS volunteers going to Creil in the summer of 1975 to dismantle and bring the Fortress back to Duxford. Reassembly took some months and in 1978 the IWM purchased the B-17 from Ted White's company. It became the major project for Ted Hagger and Eddie West, who were the first experienced aircraft engineers to join the IWM staff at Duxford, with DAS member Cliff Bishop, another qualified engineer.

The intention to return the B-17 to its original combat configuration was frustrated by the lack of gun turrets and many internal fittings. Windows installed in the fuselage during civil use were removed and the faired-over tail gun position rebuilt. In order to give maximum protection against corrosion the bomber was given a coat of paint representative of the olive drab and neutral grey used on USAAF aircraft. It had also been decided that the aircraft would be painted to represent an actual B-17G of the Eighth Air Force. However, like all B-17s produced in the last few months of the war 44-83735 had a bare metal finish and incorporated a distinctive tail gun position known as the Cheyenne. Very few camouflaged Eighth Air Force B-17s had this type of tail turret and this limited the selection. In fact, photographic cover on only two suitable identities were found and of these a 615th Bomb Squadron machine called *Mary Alice* was selected. When the history of the real *Mary Alice* was researched, it was found that the choice could not have been more appropriate as a representation of combat durability of a B-17.

Locating and purchasing and installing the missing equipment in *Mary Alice* took many years although externally, once painted, the aircraft looked complete. Missing components were obtained from US dealers, some through the assistance of the 8th Air Force Memorial Museum Foundation. The last major component to be installed was a genuine top turret in 1996. The correct model Sperry is exceptionally rare and the IWM was only able to purchase a badly damaged and corroded example from the US. It took five years work by DAS members Graham Douglas, Steve Bones and Andy Lantsbury to repair and fully equip the turret. Many missing parts had to be manufactured.

The real *Mary Alice* was so named for his mother by its first assigned pilot Lt Dan Knight. A B-17G-35-BO, serial 42-31983, squadron code IY-G, it flew at least 98 combat missions between March 1944 and May 1945 while based at Deenethorpe, Northamptonshire with the 401st Bomb Group. Used by a number of crews the bomber sustained major damage on several occasions and it is believed that no other Eighth Air Force B-17 received so much punishment and continued in service. One crewman was killed in action flying in *Mary Alice* and others were wounded, a navigator receiving a Distinguished Service Cross, the second highest US award for bravery and the only one to a member of the 401st Bomb Group.

Opposite page: Summer 1987 saw three B-17s on the Duxford apron. The occasion was the imminent departure of another ex-IGN B-17 to the USA, piloted by Jeffrey Ethell. This Fortress, the centre aircraft, had been refurbished and painted in 303rd Bomb Group colours by Stephen Gray's organisation for an American buyer. The far aircraft is *Sally B* in her 447th Bomb Group decor, and the nearest *Mary Alice*, which at that time sported a dummy top turret. (DUX 87-27-27)

Below: A DAS member at work on No 1 engine nacelle during 1981. It took eleven years to bring the Fortress back to its original configuration and then only externally. The delay was simply the difficulty of finding parts to replace those that had been removed to fashion the aircraft's more peaceable roles. (IWM 81-21-6)

Crew	Ten.
Engines	Four 1,200 hp (895 kW) Wright R-1820 radials with turbochargers.
Dimensions	Wing span 103 ft 9 in (31.62 m). Length 74ft 4 in (22.78 m).
Weight	36,135 lb empty (16,391 kg). 72,000 lb (32,659 kg) full load.
Armament	Thirteen 0.50 in machine guns. Maximum bomb load 17,600 lb (7,983 kg). Average bomb load 4,000-5,000 lb (1,814-2,268 kg).
Performance	Top speed 300 mph (482 kph) at 30,000 ft (9,150 m). Cruise speed 180 mph (289 kph). Service ceiling 35,000 ft (10,850). Combat range 2,000 miles (3,218 km) with 4,000 lb (1,814 kg) of bombs.

The real *Mary Alice* was probably the most battle scared B-17 to serve with the Eighth Air Force, yet it survived near a hundred combat missions and was flown back to the USA at the end of hostilities. Much of this endurance was due to crew chief M/Sgt. Henry McKinney and his team who kept the bomber airworthy. The photograph shows the many 'silver' tail parts that replaced the camouflaged painted originals damaged by enemy action.

North American F-100D Super Sabre

With the broadening of the Duxford collection to include all American military and naval aircraft of note, the opportunity arose early in 1976 to obtain an F-100D Super Sabre. Originally designed as a supersonic air superiority fighter the Super Sabre was given a chiefly tactical role in service with the USAF. The first production aircraft came from the Inglewood, California plant during summer 1953 although unforeseen technical difficulties delayed large scale acceptance for two years until modifications were incorporated and improved models became available. The last F-100, the 2,270th, left the second source factory at Columbus, Ohio in 1959. Super Sabres were used extensively by the USAF during the Vietnam conflict and during the 1960s was the major fighter type in the USAF element of NATO forces. F-100s served with the 20th and 48th Tactical Fighter Wings at UK bases for periods between May 1957 and April 1972. Denmark, France, Turkey and Taiwan were loaned F-100s withdrawn from USAF units.

The aircraft secured by Duxford, serial 54-2165, was accepted from the manufacturer by the USAF on 26 May 1956. An F-100D-10-NA model, it later underwent

Opposite page: Pilot 1st Lt. Robert Sampsel about to board 54-2165 at Chaumont, France in 1957. At that time the F-100D was assigned to the 493rd Fighter Bomber Squadron, 48th Fighter Bomber Wing, which had a mission of tactical nuclear weapon delivery. The 493rd insignia can be seen just below the cockpit. *Ben R Fuller*

Above: As found at Sculthorpe in the colours of Escadron 2/11. (DX 11)

systems modifications to be redesignated as an F-100D-11-NA. Flown to Europe it was assigned to the 493rd Tactical Fighter Squadron, 48th Tactical Fighter Wing based at Chaumont, France early in 1957, remaining with the unit until 1959. Primary mission of this squadron was tactical nuclear weapon delivery. After complete overhaul at Getafe, Spain, it was passed to the French Air Force and entered service with Escadron I/3 in March 1959 at Rheims. While with this unit it carried the code 3-IG on the fuselage. In December 1965 this F-100 was transferred to Escadron 2/11 at Toul, remaining with this unit until 1975. While with 2/11 the aircraft hit a stop barrier after failing to become airborne on 5 September 1968 sustaining damage to wings, undercarriage and fuselage.

Returned to the USAF, 54-2165 was flown to RAF Sculthorpe on 24 November 1975 where the 7519th CSS prepared it for storage. The aircraft had amassed a total of 4001 flying hours during its service with USAF and French units. Surplus to USAF requirements it was donated on permanent loan to the IWM, who arranged for dismantling and road transport to Duxford where it arrived on 17 May 1976.

F-100D serial number 54-2165 was parked outdoors for a number of years still sporting the Armée de l' Air colours. Earmarked for the American Air Museum building, in 1991 IWM conservation officers Chris Knapp and Paul Rushen were assigned to the aircraft as their major restoration project. The canopy and ejector seat were removed, cleaned and treated against corrosion. The airframe was paint stripped and prepared for repainting. After overhauling the undercarriage the tyres were inflated with Tyrfil, a process using a synthetic rubber compound to protect against the explosive danger of high pressure tyres on deteriorating rims. Where needed, corrosion treatment was carried out. A delaying factor in completing the restoration was the inability to obtain the original type panel fasteners, resulting in some 2,000 re-drillings of securing points. Resprayed early in 1992 the Super Sabre was finished in the markings carried by an aircraft of the 352nd Tactical Fighter Squadron, 35th Tactical Fighter Wing while operating in the South-East Asia conflict.

Weighing nearly ten short tons, the F-100 is the heaviest of the aircraft suspended from the roof and the first to be so placed. It is positioned in a diving attitude.

Parked in a Duxford hangar - although through shortage of space often outside - the F-100 remained in its Armée de l'Air markings for more than 15 years. (DXP(T) 86-10-12)

Commencement of spraying a camouflage pattern in Hangar 1, early 1992. Plastic sheeting protects from dust, bird droppings and other spray drift. (DXP 92-37-1)

Natural metal finish during its USAF and FAF operational service, the F-100D's Vietnam era paint scheme also acts as a protective coating. (DXP 92-62-7)

Crew	One.
Engines	One 16,950 lb (75.4 kN) static thrust Pratt & Whitney J57-P-21A turbojet with afterburning.
Dimensions	Wing span 39 ft (11.89 m). Length 49 ft (14.95 m).
Weight	20,638 lb (9,361 kg) empty. 39,750 lb (18,030 kg) take off.
Armament	Four fixed forward firing 20 mm M39E cannon in forward fuselage and up to 7,040 lb (3,193 kg) of bombs, rockets or missiles.
Performance	Maximum speed Mach 1.3 (about 908 mph, 1,461 kph). Cruising speed 578 mph (944 kph) at 36,000 ft (10,973 m). Service ceiling 47,700 ft (14,548 m). Combat range 1,060 miles (1,705 km).

North American B-25J Mitchell

Duxford Aviation Society members in the process of dismantling the B-25 at Shoreham in August 1976. The specially moulded nose transparency remained intact despite the derelict state of the aircraft.

Much of the early restoration was also carried out by a team of DAS members. A notable achievement was fashioning a new nose as that of the original factory production structure. (IWM 81-30-35)

The B-25, designed by North American Aviation in 1939, entered service with the USAAF two years later. Rated as a medium bomber it proved a dependable machine devoid of handling vices. In total 9,815 were built in many versions, the type also serving with the US Navy and Marine Corps, RAF and Commonwealth, Chinese, Soviet and Netherlands air forces during the Second World War and with other air forces subsequently. The name Mitchell was given in honour of General Billy Mitchell, whose early advocacy of air power ultimately cost him his career in the US Army. The most famous operation involving Mitchells was the carrier-launched raid on Tokyo in April 1942. Its leader Lt Colonel Jimmy Doolittle, was later promoted to command the Eighth Air Force in the UK. Although a group of USAAF B-25s was based in England for a few weeks, before moving on to North Africa, the type was never employed on bombing operations from the UK by American forces. The RAF used the Mitchell for bombing and had four of its squadrons affording tactical support to ground forces following the cross-Channel invasion. Twelve B-25 squadrons comprised part of the US Twelfth Air Force in the Mediterranean war zones but the largest USAAF use of Mitchell was in the war with Japan involving 26 squadrons.

The Duxford Mitchell, B-25J-30-NC serial number 44-31171, was manufactured at Kansas City in March/April 1945 and accepted by the USAAF on the 17th of the latter month. The aircraft went straight into storage at Laurel Field, Mississippi where it remained until early November the same year. Having been removed from storage and serviced, it was ferried to Lake Charles Field, California on 6 November and there held by the 307th Air Base Unit. Used primarily for pilot proficiency flights, in recognition of its trainer status, it was redesignated as a TB-25J in September 1946. On 27 January 1947 44-31171 was transferred to the 4000th Air Base Unit at Wright-Patterson AFB where it was used to conduct equipment trials. The aircraft remained at Wright-Patterson for ten years, during that time serving other units and being redesignated thrice; as an EB-25J, ETB-25J and lastly a JTB-25J. In July 1957, with more than 2,400 flying hours, this Mitchell was deemed time expired for experimental

work, flown to the Davis-Monthan storage base and removed from the USAF inventory in October. 31171 was not long in the desert. Registered for civil use as N7614C, in April 1958 the aircraft was purchased by Ace Smelting Inc, of San Antonio, Texas, presumably for the metal. However, the aircraft was not destroyed as more profitable disposal was found six months later. The inherent stability of the Mitchell made it a popular type for specialist use by commercial organisations and 44-31171 was sold on to the Radio Corporation of America, New Jersey, for use by its Defence Electronics Products Division to test various radar/electronic devices. After overhaul by Atlantic Aviation the Mitchell was usually based at New Castle, Delaware. For experimental employment the aircraft was subject to much modification, most notably in April 1960 when a fibreglass nose was installed to carry electronics and a gunner's riding seat fitted in the rear fuselage. The CG was effected by the placement of this equipment requiring the 200 lb of ballast previously installed to be moved rearwards 30 inches. Further extensive modifications were carried out in September 1962 although specialised electronic and associated equipment was frequently changed throughout RCA's use of the aircraft. A decision to retire the Mitchell from this work, saw all

When HRH Queen Elizabeth, the Queen Mother paid a visit to Duxford on 6 July 1985 she was introduced to several of the people who had worked on the B-25 restoration. (DUX(CN) 85-6-15)

Mitchells served widely with the US armed forces: 386BG flew B-26s, these operated over Italy. *US National Archives*

experimental equipment removed from the aircraft by the end of 1963. Passing into the ownership of Pennsylvania State University on 2 January 1964, six months later it was bought by a dealership, Jack Adams Aircraft Sales Inc, of Walls, Mississippi, for H W Harbican of Houston, Texas. January 1966 saw N7614C sold to Continental Aircraft Sales of Medford, New Jersey and registered in the name of Flying W Productions Inc. This organisation used it as an aerial platform for filming, having a special moulded nose transparency fitted by Longhorn Airways of Medford in July 1957.

The pilot trader Jeff Hawke became involved in securing aircraft for various motion picture productions, buying N7614C as a camera vehicle. In 1969 the Mitchell came to the UK for use in filming *Mosquito Squadron* and a promotional film for BOAC. During trans-Atlantic movement and operation in the UK the Mitchell continued to sport the US civil identity as it was registered to Euramericair of Fort Lauderdale, Hawke's company. For a

while it reposed at Luton and was then, allegedly, impounded at Prestwick during an attempted return to the USA. A further impounding at Dublin airport brought rumours of clandestine employment. In 1974 the Mitchell arrived and languished at Shoreham, its registration certificate being withdrawn at the end of October 1975. There was a move to sell the aircraft for scrap until, in August 1976, Jeff Hawke offered the aircraft to the IWM as a gift. Once more the DAS volunteers were involved and commencing on 21 August the Mitchell was dismantled during the following weeks with the final load arriving at Duxford on 29 November 1976.

Restoration of this much modified airframe took many years. A DAS team under John Kidby carried out much of the early work, fashioning a completely new nose to replace the ungainly piece fitted for air filming. However, other priorities, shortage of components and loss of team members, brought work to a standstill in the early 1980's and little was done on the project for several years. With its planned inclusion in the American Air Museum, two IWM engineers, Eric Perrott and Martin Barnes, were given the Mitchell as their major project from summer 1991. At that time it was expected to take two years to complete; tail, rear fuselage, main planes and engines all having to be overhauled and fitted and a rear gun position manufactured. The task was helped along by the FFV Aerotech apprentices who carried out some of the anti-corrosion work. Even so completion took much longer than anticipated, the joining of all major components not being achieved until 1995. As with all warplanes turned to civil use gun turrets were missing. Fortunately, the correct upper type was located in the US, being one of the last major items fitted in 1996. The final pieces, side gun positions and dummy guns, were not installed until the Mitchell was in the new building.

In order to give recognition to all US flying services of the Second World War, the decision was taken to paint 44-31171 to represent an aircraft of the Marine Corps. The US Navy received 706 B-25Js for use by the Marine Corps which in its system of designations became PBJs. Seven Marine squadrons were formed with the type and saw service in Pacific area of operations, 45 PBJs being lost in combat.

Crew	Six.
Engines	Two 1,700 hp (1,268 kW) Wright R-2600 radials.
Dimensions	Wing span 67 ft 7 in (20.5 m). Length 53ft 5¾ in (16.3 m).
Weight	19,480 lb (8,836 kg) empty. 35,000 lb (15,876 kg) full load.
Armament	Twelve 0.50 in machine guns. Maximum 6,000 lb (2,721kg) bombs.
Performance	Maximum speed 285 mph (458 kph) at 13,000 ft (3,965 m). Cruising speed 230 mph (370 kph). Service ceiling 24,200 ft (7,381 m). Combat range 1,200 miles (1,931 km) with 3,200 lb (1,451 kg).

Masking the nose ready for spraying, early 1996. (DUX 96-4-6)

In position in the American Air Museum and representative of US Marine Corps aviation. (DUX CN 97-1-49)

Grumman TBM-3 Avenger

Grumman Aircraft Corporation produced some of the best ship-board aircraft of the Second World War, the Avenger being no exception. The name stemmed from a determination to avenge the December 1941 Japanese attack on Pearl Harbor which brought the United States into the war. Avengers totalled 9,836 including 2,290 TBF models built by Grumman, the majority being produced by the General Motors Eastern Division plant at Trenton, New Jersey under the designation TBM. Designed as a torpedo bomber its internal weapons bay could also hold a 2,000 bomb or depth charges. Later models could also carry wing mounted rockets for air-to-surface use. Main defensive armament, a powered turret with a single .50 machine gun, was the first such installation on a single engine US warplane. US Navy Avengers played a part in the sinking of at least 60 Japanese naval vessels, including the giant battleships *Yamato* and *Musashi*. The Royal Navy received 958 Avengers and some saw action from carriers of the Royal Navy's Pacific Fleet. The Avenger's spacious weapons bay lent itself to housing sea-search radars and other electronic equipment, a number so converted serving with both navies well into the 1950s.

The IWM's TBM-3E model was built in 1944 as US Navy Bureau serial 69327. Supplied to the Royal Canadian Navy it became number 326 although little is known about the aircraft's service history. The carrying capacity of the type made it popular for specialised civil use, particularly fire fighting and crop spraying. In a civilian role it was first employed on spraying against budworm in British Columbian forests. It was then modified for fire fighting. While thus employed by Conair of Abbotsford, Vancouver, The TBM suffered an accident and was sufficiently damaged to be unworthy of repair, becoming an insurance write-off. Shipped to the UK in November 1977, the aircraft arrived at Duxford under the identity of its Canadian civil registration CF-KCG. Requiring major repair, the aircraft was put into long term storage. The realisation that the then incumbent of the White House, President George Bush, was a US Navy TBM pilot during the Second World War, offered an opportunity for good publicity for the American Air Museum project. The plan was to ask the President for permission to paint the Duxford example in the markings worn by his wartime aircraft. This led to a priority restoration job in spring 1990. The damaged nose section, which included the cowlings and dishpan, had to be rebuilt. Corrosion treatment was

As flying tanker No 15 in Conair service, CF-KCG was used for forest fire fighting. Over Ontario in the photograph, the pilot was Les Makis and the other crew member John Holmgreen. (J Holmgreen)

given to the fuselage. The starboard wing had been broken in the crash but a replacement, albeit in poor condition, had been obtained in the US as also had a turret, a component that had been discarded when the aircraft was converted for civil use. Although much work still had to be carried out the Avenger was painted up in appropriate US Navy colours so that Senator John Tower, the Chairman of the US Appeal, could perform a 'christening' ceremony for the cameras in June 1990.

Conservation continued during the following year with the crew canopy being returned to its original configuration and repairs were made to the port wing which had also suffered in the accident. By the winter of 1992-93 the starboard wing was ready for attaching to the fuselage and the task of manufacturing bomb-bay doors undertaken. These had been removed in Canada to allow spray tanks to be installed and making new ones from scratch took Ron Smouton, the contractor involved, a year. Help was forthcoming from Avro International at Woodford whose apprentices made an aileron for the Avenger. Although structurally complete to meet the deadline for suspending in the new building, small detail additions were added when the Avenger was in place. Prior to being installed a completely new paint job had been carried out with the pilot credit Lt George Bush and the name Barbara for his wife.

CF-KCG's flying days came to an end with a take-off crash in 1975? The starboard wing sustained the most damage.
J Holmgreen

Duxford conservation officers Chris Knapp and Sid Watkinson with volunteer helpers attaching a restored wing, summer 1993 in hangar 5. (DXP CN 93-54-10)

Finishing touches during final phase of reconstruction in 1996. Martin Barnes fixing rivets. (DXP CN 96-77-17)

Crew	Three.
Engine	One 1,900 hp (1,417 kW) Wright R-2600-20 radial.
Dimensions	Wing span 54ft 2 in (16.51 m). Length 40ft 11 in (12.48 m).
Weight	10,545 lb (4,783 kg) empty. 17,895 lb (8,117 kg) full load.
Armament	Four 0.50 machine guns. One torpedo or up to 2,000 lb (907 kg) of bombs. Up to eight air-to-surface rockets.
Performance	Maximum speed 276 mph (444 kph) at 16,000 ft (4,880 m). Cruise speed 147 mph (236 kph). Service ceiling 25,000 ft (7,625 m). Combat range 1,000 miles (1,609 km).

After painting in the colours of the TBM flown by George Bush when serving in the US Navy in 1945. Conservation officers Geoff Cousins and John White stopped work on vehicle projects to carry out this work. (DXP CN 96-66-5)

Suspended in the American Air Museum. (DXP CN 96-1-1028)

Lockheed T-33

An advanced jet trainer, the T-33 was basically a two-seat development of the P-80 Shooting Star, America's first jet fighter to enter operational service. In total 5,811 T-33s were built by Lockheed and the type was also built under licence in Canada and Japan. The T-33 remained the USAF's standard transitional jet trainer for over 15 years. Through the Mutual Defence Assistance Program set up by the USA to re-arm NATO countries during the Cold War threat, T-33A serial number 51-4286 was transferred for French use soon after acceptance by the USAF in March 1952. The aircraft served at least ten different units of the Armée de l'Air during the following 26 years being returned to the USAF in 1978. It is known to have been involved in one accident involving nose wheel damage while being operated by unit BE708 on 10 September 1956. A total of 95 T-33As were supplied to the French, who allocated two for training at each base with a strike or fighter commitment.

Flown to Sculthorpe and surplus to USAFE requirements, ejection seats were disarmed and fuel and hydraulic systems purged, before the aircraft was given on indefinite loan to the IWM in 1978. The recovery team from Duxford commenced dismantling work the following March although the main concentration of effort took place during the first week of April in generally atrocious weather. To remove the wing, which had to be lowered in one piece, the fuselage first had to be raised by jacking and supported on drums. Four hydraulic jacks were then used to slowly lower the wing, a procedure that took two hours. Loaded onto two vehicles the aircraft was delivered to Duxford on 8 April 1979.

The T-33 was stored for thirteen years until earmarked for the American Air Museum. Restoration work started in 1991 under Bevis Griffiths and Andy Robinson. All major components were removed, inspected and where necessary made ready for corrosion treatment by bead blasting. Delays in effecting this processing brought work virtually to a standstill the following year. Restoration work was restarted in 1993 with Sid Watkinson replacing Bevis Griffiths, only to halt when these engineers were diverted to another project.

However, in the spring of 1994 a concerted effort was made to complete the renovation of the T-33 – this time in the hands of Andy Robinson – in the knowledge that this would be one of the aircraft to be suspended from the roof. Even so, there was some diversion of effort to work on the B-52 in 1995. Restoration was completed by the following spring with a complete respray. The T-33 is finished in a scheme appropriate to USAF service.

Arrival at Duxford from Sculthorpe, 8 April 1979. (John Kidby)

Crew	Two.
Engine	One 5,200 lb (23.3 kN) static thrust Allison J33-A-35 turbojet.
Dimensions	Wing span 38 ft 10½ in (11.85 m). Length 37 ft 9 in (11.51 m).
Weight	8,084 lb (3,667 kg) empty. 11,965 lb (5,427 kg) loaded.
Armament	Two 0.50 machine guns. Provision for underwing munitions.
Performance	Maximum speed 590 mph (950 kph). Service ceiling 47,500 ft (14,480 m). Range 1,345 miles (2,164 km).

A boom crane lowers the refurbished forward fuselage onto the wing, summer 1996. Chris Knapp (left) and Tanva Boulder are the staff members overseeing this delicate operation. (DUX CN 96-44-8)

Resplendent in USAF markings the T-33 hangs from the museum roof. (DUX 96-1-936)

Boeing B-29 Superfortress

Apart from a lone visitor in the spring of 1944, the B-29 Superfortress was not seen in Europe during the Second World War. Of greater size, range, speed and warload capacity than any other mass produced heavy bomber, the B-29 was used in a strategic bombing campaign against Japan. Commencing operations from India in June 1944 with a raid on Bangkok, by the following summer the operating agency, the 20th Air Force, had a force of almost a thousand in 62 squadrons at bases on the Marianas in the Pacific. Employing low-level incendiary night attacks Japanese industrial centres were devastated. The campaign was terminated by the dropping of the two atomic bombs, on Hiroshima and Nagasaki. Total 20th Air Force B-29 losses were 118 through enemy air action and 216 to other causes. Entering production late in 1941, a total of 3,960 Superfortresses were built by four plants.

Following the cessation of hostilities the B-29 was the main conveyance for the USAAF/USAF atomic deterrent until speedier bombers entered service in the 1950s. It was used in a tactical role with conventional bombs during the Korean War of 1950-53 and 88 were supplied to the RAF which needed an advanced heavy bomber prior to the arrival of their jet powered V-bombers. Several USAF B-29s were modified for use in air-to-air in-flight refuelling.

The Duxford Superfortress, the only museum example in Europe, is a B-29A-BN, serial number 44-61748 built at Renton, Washington and delivered to Birmingham air depot, Alabama on 26 May 1945. It was apparently never assigned to an operational unit during the last months of the Second World War. First held as a possible combat replacement by the 421st Base Unit at Muroc, California from June to November 1945, the bomber was then moved to the 410th Base Unit at Davis-Monthan, Arizona for long term storage. With the outbreak of the Korean War and the expansion of Strategic Air Command, 44-61748 was taken out of storage in June 1951 and flown to Luke AFB, Arizona where it was held by the 3040th Aircraft Storage Squadron until the following February when it was delivered to Travis AFB, California and readied by the 9th Bomb Group for despatch to the Far East Air Force Bomber Command (Provisional). Although

despatched to the FEAF in the spring of 1952, apparently the aircraft was not assigned to the 371st Bomb Squadron of the 307th Bomb Group (later Wing) at Kadena, Okinawa until 1 August. Soon adorned with a razorback boar motif and the name *It's Hawg Wild*, the bomber in 1952 took part in night operations over North

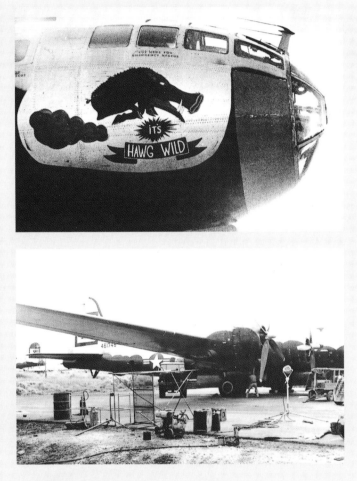

It's Hawg Wild, the slogan-cum-nickname bestowed on B-29A 44-61748 by men of the 371st Bomb Squadron, 307th Bomb Wing in 1952. (HU39033)

On the flight line at Kadena, Okinawa, September 1952. Yellow nose band identified the 371st Bomb Squadron with the 307th Bomb Wing. At the time Strategic Air Command identified its bomber and reconnaissance wings by a letter within a geometrical shape. Y was the 307th Bomb Wing and the square showed the wing was under the 2nd Air Force when based in the USA. (HU39014)

Korea against communications and supply centres reportedly completing 36 sorties. When the 307th returned to the US in November 1954 its B-29s were placed in storage at Davis-Monthan AFB, under the 3040th Aircraft Storage Squadron. Here 44-61748 was taken out of first line service and the following March flown to the Nashville repair facility, Tennessee for overhaul and modification for training duties and then on to Tinker AFB, Oklahoma for additional work. Redesignated as a TB-29A, in July 1955 the bomber was allocated to the 4750th Air Defence Wing at Yuma County Airport, Arizona where it was used primarily for target towing. Surplus to USAF requirements, in November 1956 the aircraft was passed to the US Marine Corps who

---

Opposite page:

Top: Engine start, 16 November 1979, for the third attempted take-off from the Naval Weapons Center, China Lake. The first attempt two days earlier was aborted due to fuel pump trouble. After changing the faulty fuel pump a second attempt to become airborne on 15 November was abandoned due to a pronounced swing to port. After adjustments the third try proved successful and the bomber flew to Tucson without serious problems. (HU38457)

Centre left: It is said that 4,000 people came to watch the Superfortress land at Duxford on 2 March 1980. The approach was made over the M11 motorway. (IWM 80-4-71)

Centre right: The delivery crew at Duxford. Jack Kern, on the far right, masterminded the whole rescue and overhaul operation at China Lake and Tucson, as well as acting as flight engineer on the delivery flight. On the left of the picture is Skip Creiger who piloted the B-29, and who lost his life in a light aircraft crash shortly after his return to the USA. In addition to the flight crew another five people, including three women, were on board when the aircraft arrived at Mildenhall. The insignia on the right side of the nose is that of the 42nd Bomb Wing which, together with the SAC emblem on the left side, appeared after the overnight stay at Loring AFB, the 42nd's home. (IWM 80-4-77)

Bottom: Initial restoration at Duxford during the early 1980s was limited to dealing with external corrosion and a paint job in the markings worn while with the 307th Bomb Wing in Okinawa. (MH27010)

employed it on similar work at the Naval Weapons Center, China Lake, California. Retired from target towing the B-29 remained parked at China Lake for the next 23 years.

With IWM interest in obtaining a B-29 the US Navy gave the aircraft on indefinite loan, the official transfer dating from 27 September 1979. Although stored in the open there had been practically no corrosion of the airframe due to the arid desert conditions at China Lake. In the spring of 1979 an IWM team under Geoff Bottomley went out to conduct an examination of eight B-29s at China Lake and selected 44-61748 as being in the best condition. On the advice of John Kern, an aviation engineer from Tucson , Arizona, rather than disassemble the aircraft a decision was taken to fly it to the UK. Preparatory work by Kern took seven months, but after three attempts the B-29 was finally flown out of China Lake for Tucson on 13 November

1979. More work by Kern at his Tucson base and the aircraft took off on the first stage of its flight to the UK on 16 February 1980, by way of Flint (Michigan), Loring AFB (Maine), Gander (Newfoundland), Sondrestrom (Greenland), Keflavik (Iceland), arriving at Mildenhall on 1 March, then on to Duxford on the 2nd. The failure of a specially installed heater on the stage between Newfoundland and Greenland - 24 February - made the flight deck so cold that the crew, all suffering some degree of exposure, had to be taken to hospital in Sondrestrom to be thawed out.

Although external paintwork was worn the tail insignia of the 307th Bomb Wing, a letter Y in an outline rectangle, was still visible on the tail, as was the name and insignia for *Hawg Wild*. Being such a large aircraft and with sheltered accommodation at Duxford limited, the Superfortress was mostly parked outdoors. Unfortunately the dust and sand lodged in the airframe by dry desert winds then began to collect moisture and precipitate corrosion. Restoration was protracted, although the FFV Aerotech (taken over by FLS Aerospace) apprentices from Stansted made a major contribution to tackling the internal corrosion in the rear bomb bay area where the main deterioration was located on the Superfortress in 1991. The following year the FLS apprentices continued

Although the exterior looked good, as this 1984 photograph shows, the flight deck was somewhat worn. (DXP[T] 84-26-31)

Pilots' outlook from a B-29 was excellent in comparison with other bombers of its day. (DXP[T] 92-73-2)

their corrosion repairs concentrating on the undercarriage bays and the rear fuselage sections. Much more had to be done but due to more pressing work it was not until the summer of 1995 that a determined effort to complete restoration could be mounted. Robin Cutting, a newly recruited temporary conversation officer, was put in charge. Still existing corrosion was dealt with in the aft fuselage, undercarriage and bomb-bays and the aircraft was repositioned in No 1 hangar for painting. During the spring of 1996 the bomb-bay doors and wingtips were refitted as was the internal equipment previous removed to allow anti-corrosion work. The battle against corrosion was not over, for inspection of the rudder revealed damage to the rear spar. Removal, treatment and repair followed. After refitting the rear upper turret and adding dummy gun barrels where required, the whole aircraft was paint stripped, primed and resprayed ready for moving into the American Air Museum. The Superfortress carries its true identity, retaining its *Hawg Wild* decor of the Korean War plus yellow training bands of later days.

Crew	Eleven.
Engines	Four 2,200 hp (1,641 kW) Wright R-3350 radials with turbochargers.
Dimensions	Wing span 142 ft 3 in (43.4 m). Length 99 ft (30.19 m).
Weight	71,500 lb (32,432 kg) empty. 140,000 lb (63,504 kg) maximum load.
Armament	Twelve 0.50 in calibre machine guns. Maximum bomb load (short range) 20,000 lb (9,072 kg). Normal bomb load 5,000 - 12,000 lb (2,268 kg - 5,443 kg).
Performance	Maximum speed 399 mph (642 kph) at 30,000 ft (9,150 m). Cruising speed 230 mph (370 kph). Service ceiling 39.650 ft (12,093 m). Combat range 4,000 miles (6,436 km) with 5,000 lb (2,268 kg) bomb load.

Douglas C-47 Skytrain

The Duxford C-47 had a variety of identities during its flying life. Constructor's number 19975, it was 43-15509 in the USAAF, SE-BBH as a Swedish air liner, N9985F and later N51V on the US civil register, T3-29 with the Spanish air force, G-BHUB on the British register and a bogus G-AGIV for the television 'soap' Airline. The struggles of the fictional Ruskin Air Services to survive in early post-war air transport operations was the basis of the 1980 TV series staring Roy Marsden. *Ken Pettit*

C-47 was the USAAF designation for its most numerous military version of the most successful of all propeller driven air transports. Based on the DC-3 airliner of 1935, the wartime production of all variants, including US Navy models, totalled 10,048. Reliable with good cargo capacity, the C-47 could carry a 7,500 lb load or up to 28 fully armed troops. The type served with the USAAF in all war zones and was also supplied to the RAF, Commonwealth and Allied air forces. The largest contingent formed the IX Troop Carrier Command, a thousand aircraft in 56 squadrons. From bases in England these C-47s transported troops and equipment for the airborne invasions of Normandy and the Low Countries in June and September 1944 respectively. Using mostly continental airfields C-47s were the main type involved in the airborne assault for the Rhine crossing in the following March.

Although officially called Skytrain in USAAF service this was rarely heard. Post-war, when more than sixty air forces world-wide came to use the C-47 the RAF name, Dakota, became the common tag.

With large numbers surplus to US military requirements from 1946, the C-47 became the popular workhorse of many small airlines and freight carriers, remaining so for best part of a half century. Relatively cheap to purchase, easy to maintain and operate no other transport had such worldwide employment. It played an important part in the Berlin Airlift and was returned to military use as a gunship during the Vietnam War.

The American Air Museum has a C-47A-85-DL model, serial number 43-15509, built by Douglas at its Long Beach, California plant and accepted by the USAAF in April 1944. Flown to the UK the following month it served for a year with 37th Troop Carrier Squadron of the 316th Troop Carrier Group at Cottesmore. The aircraft took part in the D-Day operations of 6 June, the airborne invasion of Holland and possibly the 24 March Rhine crossing. Following the 316th Group's return to the USA, 43-15509 was sold to the Swedish airline ABA, registered as SE-BBH and named *Vraken Viking*. Transferred to SAS, with a name change to *Helge Viking*, it was returned to

America in the early 1950s under the US registration N9985F. The aircraft next appeared serving Piedmont Aviation Inc., in 1953 with registration N51V and went to Charlotte Aircraft Corporation in April 1962. The next operator was the Spanish Air Force where this C-47 served as a personnel transport. In 1980 the aircraft was bought by Aces High Ltd for use in the fictional TV series *Airline*. When this company came to dispose of the Dakota later that year it was obtained by the IWM. The aircraft was completely repainted using the code W7-S and markings similar to those carried while assigned to the 37th Troop Carrier Squadron at Cottesmore.

C-47 Skytrains of the 37th Troop Carrier Squadron ready to tow off an armada of Waco CG-4A assault gliders at Cottesmore, 1944. *via Roy Bonser*

The paint job given the C-47 in the early 1980s was completely removed in 1996 and the aircraft treated with anti-corrosion materials. The aircraft was photographed in No 5 hangar prior to repainting in the same 316th TCG scheme. It is believed these were the same code markings carried while operating from Cottesmore in 1944. (DUX 96-10-34)

Paul Rushen engaged in the tricky task of installing the propeller on No 2 engine following respraying, summer 1996. (DUX CN 96-55-8)

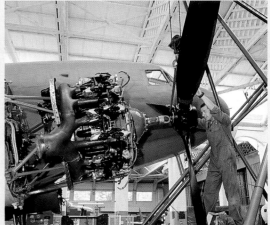

Refurbishment of the C-47 to ready it for the American Air Museum did not begin until the spring of 1992. Earlier that year the rudder and tailplane sustained damage during a very high wind, the aircraft having spent most of its early years at Duxford parked outdoors. In the summer Bevis Griffiths and Andy Robinson began repairs and treating the corrosion in the rear fuselage while the aircraft was still on public display. Work ceased during spring 1994 while the C-47 was used in a Duxford exhibition to mark the 50th anniversary of D-Day. On resumption of conservation tasks, wings were removed for corrosion treatment and paint stripping, fittings added in post-war years were removed and engine restoration begun. Two major areas of bad corrosion were found, the flap shroudings and the toilet. The final details – refitting of flaps, ailerons, engine cowlings and astrodome, plus a complete re-spray – were completed during the summer of 1996. As before, the markings represented those carried by the aircraft while with IX Troop Carrier Command. C-47A 43-15509, is the only aircraft in the American Air Museum that actually took part in operations from the UK during the Second World War.

Crew	Up to four.
Engines	Two 1,200 hp (895 kW) Pratt & Whitney R-1830 radials.
Dimensions	Wing span 95 ft (28.96 m). Length 63 ft 9 in (19.5 m).
Weight	16,970 lb (7,697 kg) empty. 29,300 lb (13,290 kg) full load.
Performance	Maximum speed 220 mph (354 kph) at 7,500 ft (2,287 m). Cruise speed 185 mph (296 kph) at 10,000 ft (3,050 m). Service ceiling 24,000 ft (7,320 m). Range 1,500 miles (2,400 km).

The only aircraft in the American Air Museum to actually participate in combat operations during the Second World War. In position and awaiting installation of its engine cowlings. (DUX CN 97-1-391)

Republic P-47D Thunderbolt

Largest and heaviest single-engine fighter of the Second World War to see quantity production, the P-47 Thunderbolt proved very effective in both air combat and ground attack. Despite a poor rate of climb and acceleration compared with contemporaries, its superior speed at high altitude and heavy firepower enabled US Eighth Air Force P-47 pilots to inflict heavy losses on the Luftwaffe while providing escort for heavy bombers during autumn, winter and spring 1943-44. High fuel consumption limited the P-47's range for escort duties, but the type found a new role in air support of ground forces. Rugged construction and a durable air-cooled engine enabled the Thunderbolt to better survive enemy fire than other aircraft given the same ground attack mission. The Ninth Air Force had 42 P-47 squadrons engaged in these operations supporting American armies advancing through western Europe. The Twelfth Air Force in Italy had 18 squadrons for similar duties and there were also 6 French squadrons with P-47s operating in western Europe at the end of the war. The RAF used Thunderbolts

for ground support in Burma, equipping 12 squadrons. Total P-47 production of all models amounted to 15,683, a greater number than any other American Second World War fighter.

The P-47D was the major model and the IWM example, a P-47D-40-RA, serial 45-49192, was from one of the last batch of D models built by the Evansville, Indiana plant early in 1945. Apparently the fighter was stored by Air Materiel Command at Tinker Field, Oklahoma until becoming one of the second batch of P-47s supplied to Peru in September 1952 as a result of the Rio Pact for Mutual Defence, a military assistance programme. The Fuerza Aérea del Peru maintained Thunderbolts in service for fifteen years, finally retiring the last in July 1967. Learning this, dealer and warplane enthusiast Ed Jurist of Vintage Aircraft International managed to negotiate the purchase of six complete P-47s, one of which was 45-49192, plus a quantity of spare parts from the Peruvian Air Force. Part of the deal involved the vendor's dismantling and preparing the aircraft which were then con-

veyed by merchant ship to Texas, arriving 5 August 1969. The aircraft were then stored at the Confederate Air Force installation at Harlingen, 45-49192 being restored to flying condition during 1972-73. Registered N47DD the aircraft was painted to represent a P-47D of the wartime 527th Fighter Squadron, 86th Fighter Group. In 1975 Ed Jurist sold all six to David Tallichet, a well known 'warbird' operator, 45-49192 being stored at Barstow-Daggett, California until February 1977 when it was moved to the Yesterday's Air Force at Forbes Field, Topeka. Overhauled, the aircraft was given a new paint scheme, representative of the P-47D flown by ace Dave Schilling with the 56th Fighter Group. Early in January 1980 the aircraft was bought by Robin Collard, a former B-52 pilot, of Del Rio, Texas. Unfortunately, on 9 February 1980 in the course of delivery, following an overnight stop at Tulsa, Oklahoma, 45-49192 suffered engine problems on take-off and crashed sustaining severe damage to wings and empennage. The pilot escaped without serious injury. Lifted from the crash site by helicopter the Thunderbolt finished its journey to Del Rio in a truck. In June 1980 the wreckage was sold to Jon Ward and stored at Truckee-Tahoe, Nevada. Glenn Necesary commenced a rebuild but in 1984 sold to a friend, Jim Kirby who continued the work. However, in 1985 Stephen Grey bought the aircraft which was said to be 65 to 70 per cent complete. Stephen Grey sent the Thunderbolt to Steve Hinton of Fighter Rebuilders at Chino, California. Here another fuselage was substituted for the original

As N47DD and adorned in Second World War markings representative of the 527th Fighter Squadron, 86th Fighter Group with the nickname *Grumpy*. A 1974 photograph when the aircraft was one of six ex-Peruvian Thunderbolts refurbished by Ed Jurist.

A pile of junk! The cockpit section , photographed at Duxford just after being unloaded from road transport, gives a good idea of the formidable task facing IWM engineers in rebuilding this aircraft. In fact, it involved an estimated manufacture or replacement of some 75 per cent of the finished P-47 that stands in the American Air Museum. (DX 85-36-6)

The former operator's legend and US civil registration were still to be seen on this piece of rear fuselage. (DX 85-36-4)

together with several damaged components. In fact, the rebuild took only parts of 45-49192, more of the original remaining unused. When completed Stephen Grey's Thunderbolt was brought to Duxford as part of his airworthy Fighter Collection.

The IWM sought a Thunderbolt for static display for some years but those on the market were usually airworthy or capable of restoration for flight and therefore commanded high asking prices. The availability of the 45-49192 wreck resulted from its discovery by Edward Inman during a visit to Chino in 1985. The lot received at Duxford was somewhat disappointing, the extent of destruction being much more severe than hitherto appreciated as when viewed at Chino much of the wreckage was boxed. The fuselage was in reasonable condition but many parts of both wings were missing or beyond repair. Purchased from Stephen Grey for $60,000, it was estimated that the rebuild would cost between $120,000 and $150,000. The 8th Air Force Memorial Museum Foundation contributed $10,000 of the purchase price and later provided $20,000 towards the renovation. Work was started on the fuselage in 1987 using one of the smaller engineering buildings, albeit that progress was very slow due to irregular help from volunteer labour. Apart from the long and laborious job of straightening exhaust and supercharger ducting severely damaged when the aircraft crashed, and some manufacturing of parts for the tailplane, work came to a standstill by the early 1990s due to lack of mainplanes. Fortunately a port wing was obtained from the Netherlands where it had been used for airframe instructional work for several years, although completely stripped of accessories. And then a right hand wing was discovered at the French Air and Space Museum, Paris who agreed to a deal for some Lancaster parts. This was in far worse condition with over 50 per cent of the skin area needing replacement and major repairs to the main structure.

A concentrated effort then went into the restoration under Sid Watkinson although there were doubts if the amount of input necessary to bring the machine to exhibition standard would be possible in the required timescale. By the spring of 1996 with less than six months

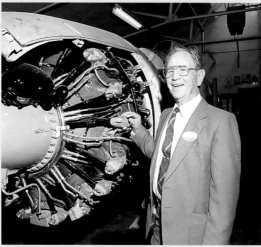

before the P-47 had to be placed in the American Air Museum building, the tailplane still had to be completed, fin, flaps, propeller, engine cowlings, undercarriage doors, wing to fuselage fairings, cockpit equipment and dummy armament had to be fitted, to say nothing of the required paint scheme. In fact, there was not time to manufacture and attach the tailplane, fin and rudder before the Thunderbolt went into the building and these together with engine cowlings, propeller and several other items had to be fitted later. Nevertheless, despite all this, the aircraft was complete with fuel drop tank and bombs attached plus dummy pilot and crew chief by the great day.

The aircraft represents P-47D serial 42-26413, *Oregon's Britannia*, the first Thunderbolt with a 180 degree vision canopy received by the 56th Fighter Group, the top scoring Eighth Air Force formation in aerial combat. The personal aircraft of the great fighter leader Colonel Hubert Zemke, 42-26413 was a presentation aircraft for operations in Britain from Oregon state, whose inhabitants subscribed the cost of a P-47 in savings bonds.

Much of the reconstruction was carried out by Ted Hagger, seen here in the process of fixing the rear fuselage which had been almost totally destroyed when the aircraft crashed. (DX 89-20-6)

Hub Zemke, one of the great fighter leaders of the Second World War, photographed when inspecting progress during his visit to Duxford on 16 September 1990. When completed the Thunderbolt was painted to represent his personal aircraft, allegedly the first with a 'bubble' canopy to see operational service in England. (DX CN 90-27-3)

P-47 crew chief Henry 'Dusty' Bauer, who was stationed at Duxford, and Sid Watkinson discuss a problem during the former's visit in 1996. There were may problems in this long and difficult reconstruction. (DX 96-56-5)

Opposite page:
The tail surfaces, like many other parts and components, were manufactured from scratch using maker's drawings. Conservation officer Sid Watkinson fixes the fin. (DX 97-18-2)

In D-Day stripes and representing the 56th Fighter Group's *Oregon's Britannia*. The finishing touches were only applied the day before the official opening of the American Air Museum by the Queen. (DX 97-1-723)

Crew	One.
Engine	One 2,300 hp (1,715 kW) Pratt & Whitney R-2800 radial with turbocharger.
Dimensions	Wing span 40 ft 9 in (12.4 m). Length 36 ft 1 in (11.03 m).
Weight	10,000 lb (4,536 kg) empty. 17,500 lb (7.938 kg) max load.
Armament	Eight 0.50 in calibre machine guns. Up to 2,000 lb (907 kg) bombs on wing racks.
Performance	Top speed 429 mph (690 kph) at 30,000 ft (9,150 m). Cruising speed 250 mph (402 kph). Service ceiling 42,000 ft (12,810 m). Combat range 250 miles (402 km) or 950 miles (1,528 km) with two 100 US gallon (377 litre) drop tanks.

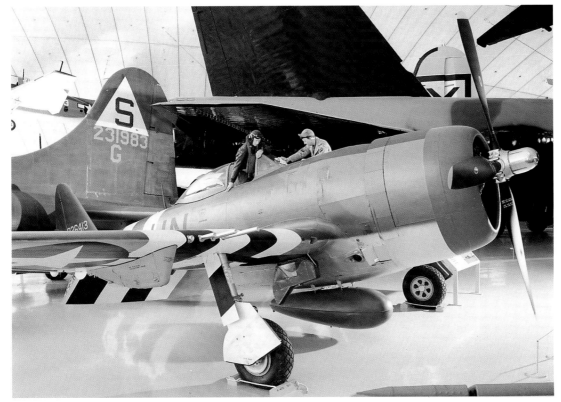

Boeing B-52 Stratofortress

Approaching a half century of service with the USAF bomber units, the B-52 has a remarkable record of durability for a first line combat aircraft. Entering service with Strategic Air Command in April 1955, a total of 744 were made in eight different models before production ceased in 1962. Originally used to carry the nuclear deterrent, B-52s were employed in the South-East Asia war of 1965-73 carrying a load of up to 30 tons of conventional bombs. B-52s were also used during the Iraqi and Balkans conflicts, some flying from Fairford in the UK. Later model B-52s are equipped to carry and launch cruise missiles.

Duxford's Stratofortress, a B-52D model serial number 56-0689, has an impressive operational history. Delivered to the USAF on 11 October 1957 by the Boeing plant at Wichita, it went to the 28th Bomb Wing at Ellsworth, South Dakota. In December 1959 the aircraft was withdrawn for overhaul at Kelly AFB, Texas. Next service was with the 4128th Strategic Wing at Amarillo AFB and the 95th Bomb Wing at Biggs AFB in Texas from February 1960 to April 1964, following which came another period of overhaul and modification at the San Antonio Air Materiel Area, Texas.

An impressive sight. The largest aircraft ever to land at Duxford on final over the M11, 8 October 1983. Police closed the motorway for a few minutes as there was some concern about safety. The pilots made a perfect touchdown and with the deployed brake parachute had ample room to bring the giant to a halt before the end of the runway. This brought the bomber's total flight time to over 14,000 hours since it first took to the air in 1957. *D White/DAS*

In June 1964 56-0689 was assigned to another SAC base in Texas, the 494th Bomb Wing at Sheppard, staying until March 1966 when again withdrawn for overhaul.

April 1966 saw a major change of location, the bomber going to the 509th Bomb Wing at Pease AFB, New Hampshire, an Eighth Air Force base. The stay was short for the following month this B-52D was sent to Douglas Aircraft, Tulsa, Oklahoma for modifications. That completed, the 91st Bomb Wing at Glasgow AFB, Montana took charge in July and in September 1966 the bomber was deployed on temporary duty at Andersen air base, Guam for nearly six months. After a year with the 91st came a transfer to the 99th Bomb Wing at Westover AFB, Massachusetts with periodic temporary duty across the Pacific to Guam and U-Tapao, Thailand for operations in South East Asia. By February 1968 another overhaul was due and following the usual excursion to San Antonio Air Materiel Area 56-0689 joined the 306th Bomb Wing at McCoy AFB, Florida in April. B-52 operations in the Vietnam area being intensified, the aircraft moved to Andersen, Guam in June 1968. Here it became a pool aircraft for use by other Bomb Wings deployed from the USA; the 454th Bomb Wing in September 1968 and the 509th in December. In January 1969 the bomber transferred to U-Tapao, Thailand for operations, the 99th Bomb Wing taking it over in September 1969. In August 1970 56-0689 returned to the USA, going to Westover AFB with the 99th, where it had served before. November 1971 saw it back to U-Tapao, still with the 99th. The bomber remained there until September 1972 when it was back to Andersen and service with the 96th Bomb Wing. Return to the USA came in November 1972 for brief service with the 7th Bomb Wing at Carswell AFB, Texas only to head back to Guam and the 99th Bomb Wing in December.

The Vietnam hostilities over, reassignments were less frequent, 56-0689 not returning to the USA until July 1973. Assigned to the 7th Bomb Wing at Carswell AFB it remained with this unit until February 1977, apart from temporary deployment to the 307th Strategic Wing at U-Tapao and 43rd Strategic Wing at Andersen from September 1974 to March 1975. The 96th Bomb Wing at Dyess AFB, Texas then inherited this B-52 where it remained until October 1982. During this period it had been deployed to Andersen, Guam under the 43rd Strategic Wing for a year from June 1978. Strategic Wings were holding units for aircraft and crews detached from regular wings. Final assignment before retirement was with the 7th Bomb Wing at Carswell, terminating in October 1983 when the USAF gave the aircraft to the RAF, reciprocating a gift of Vulcans. A 7th Wing crew flew the B-52 to Brize Norton, prior to movement to Duxford. The RAF, not having facilities to house or exhibit the aircraft, arranged for its safe-keeping with the IWM. During 26 years USAF service, 56-0689 amassed over 14,000 hours flying time and made 200 combat missions in South-East Asia.

A late production B-52D dropping a Quail decoy, designed to simulate the radar 'shape' of a Stratofortress as it penetrated enemy air space. B-52s still serve with the USAF and look set to create incredible longevity records. *Boeing*

Crew pose after the successful landing while Duxford staff fix a tow bar preparatory to towing the bomber from the runway. Left to right: Wing Commander J Herbertson, RAF Exchange Officer at Eighth Air Force HQ; Lt.Col. Wally Carpeaux, co-pilot; Major Steve Winkle, radar navigator; Lt.Col. Jim Merger, pilot; Major Joe Sihwab and Captain Wes Hewett, technical officers. (IWM 83-42-22)

Being towed past the Duxford signal square to Hangar 1, summer 1991. The aircraft, which could not be taken completely into the hangar because of the fin, was surveyed for deterioration prior to a complete refurbishment. Due to other commitments the conservation work did not take place for four years. (DXP[T] 91-34-23)

It was later discovered that the fin of a B-52 is hinged and with the proper equipment can be folded down to the right to access hangars. This facility was used in 1995 when the aircraft was taken into Hangar 1 for overhaul. (DXP 95-17-10)

With a 185 feet wing span the B-52D is not only the largest aircraft in the Duxford collection but was also the largest and heaviest aircraft to land at the airfield. The Duxford runway having been reduced to 4,500 yards length when the M11 motorway was constructed, there was concern about the safety of landing the bomber. No record existed of a B-52 using such a short runway. Precautions taken included a minimum fuel load and brief closure of the motorway section adjacent to the airfield. In the event pilot Lt Colonel James Merger touched the giant down right at the end of the runway and came to a halt without need for over-run. From the day of its arrival on 8 October 1983 the Stratofortress had to sit outside until the summer of 1991 when, preparatory to being renovated for inclusion in the American Air Museum, it was taken to No 1 'Superhangar' for a thorough survey to ascertain the deterioration suffered through seven and a half years of exposure to English weather. While No 1 hangar was the only building at Duxford wide enough to take the 185 feet span the B-52's tail height precluded the whole aircraft being accommodated. The survey found the aircraft in better condition than expected, the most corroded parts being the main fuselage longerons.

Returned to wait outdoors, some internal corrosion treatment was carried out by Eric Perrott and Martin Barnes during the next two years but the Conservation department was aware that completing renovation was the biggest single task to be undertaken during the months ahead. This started in spring 1995 with Chris Knapp co-ordinating the work. Information and equipment had been obtained for lowering the tail fin and rudder 90 degrees thus allowing complete egress to No 1 hangar, from which most other aircraft had been removed to make space for the B-52. The folding fin was a facility actually built into the structure by Boeing during manufacture. The mammoth task of paint stripping was carried out by using a dry blasting technique taking three weeks. Du Pont supplied the plastic beads for blasting which were hard enough to remove paint but soft enough not to damage the aircraft's alloy skin. Although more environmentally friendly than chemical stripping with its hazardous fumes, the process did generate considerable dust and noise causing the hangar to be closed to the public for the duration of this task. Special protective clothing had to be worn by the operatives which was far from comfortable during the hot summer weather of

1995. Further corrosion control and a complete overall respray sponsored by ICI followed before the B-52 was removed in November to once more face the winter elements. An estimated two years work had taken six months due to a concentrated effort with shift working commencing at 6.30 am and finishing at 10.30 pm, seven days a week. Only the undercarriage doors and engine cowls, needing re-skinning, were missing when the aircraft was at last rolled into the permanent cover of the new building in September 1996.

Crew	Six.
Engines	Eight Pratt & Whitney J57-P-29W turbojets each of up to 12,000 lb (53.4 kN) static thrust with water injection.
Dimensions	Wing span 185 ft (56.4 m). Length 156 ft 6 in (47.7 m). Weight 177,816 lb (80,657 kg) empty, 450,000 lb (204,120 kg) maximum.
Armament	Four 0.50 in calibre machine guns in tail. 60,000 lb (27,242 kg) bomb load.
Performance	Maximum speed 634 mph (1,020 kph) at 20,200 ft (6,161 m). Cruising speed 520 mph (837 kph). Service ceiling 46,200 ft (14,091 m). Combat range 9,237 miles (14,862 km).

Being moved to the American Air Museum after corrosion treatment and re-spraying. The formidable looking radar-controlled rear gun emplacement of the B-52 made use of the same machine gun that defended Second World War bombers, the 0.50 inch calibre Browning. (DUX 96-82-1)

McDonnell F-4 Phantom II

F-4J 155529 in the colours of VF-74, while assigned to CVW-8 and flying from USS *America* in the 1970s. (MAP, U25949)

Coming into Duxford, 10 July 1991. F-4J 155529 had become ZE359 and wore the colours of No 74 Squadron. The Phantom II was the best all-round fighter of the Cold War era. (DUX 91-18-12)

Originally designed to meet a US Navy requirement, the McDonnell F-4 had such an outstanding performance that it was ordered for the USAF as a tactical fighter. Supersonic speed capability, good endurance through large internal fuel storage and the ability to carry a heavy warload were the main qualities that saw the Phantom employed extensively in US Navy, Marine and Air Force service during two decades from the mid-1960s. A total of 5,200 were built between 1956 and 1979 including

photographic and electronic mission models. F-4s were also built under licence in Japan. The RAF had 200 Rolls-Royce powered versions and a number of F-4J models surplus to US Navy requirements. The Phantom played a major role in Vietnam operations both in air defence and ground attack. The type was used in the UK by the 10th Tactical Reconnaissance Wing at Alconbury and 81st Tactical Fighter Wing at Bentwaters.

The Phantom in the American Air Museum is an F-4J, US Navy serial number 155529, manufactured in 1967. The aircraft entered squadron service in March 1968 being assigned to VF-33 at Oceana NAS, California, and over the next few years was used by several other US Navy fighter squadrons. With VF-74 flying from the carrier USS *America* ten months were spent flying combat missions in the Vietnam war zone in 1972. With a reduction in US Navy strength this F-4J was put into storage in

1982, two years later to be one of 15 purchased by Britain to fill a need for increasing the RAF's complement of this excellent type. This came about through forming another Phantom squadron to replace that transferred from the UK to the Falklands. Refurbishment included the removal of much specialised US Navy equipment, mostly electronic, and replacement with British requirements. In August 1984 155529 was given the British iden-

tity of ZE359 and sent to No 74 Squadron which had re-formed at Wattisham. The aircraft remained with No 74 at Wattisham until 1991 when it was presented to the IWM by the Ministry of Defence.

For landing at Duxford on 10 July 1991 portable arrester gear had been set up by the RAF in case the Phantom, which did not decelerate quickly, ran out of runway. The aircraft still had the naval hook for terminating carrier landings and this was used at Duxford. Flown direct from Wattisham by Squadron Leader Dai Whittingham with Squadron Leader David Loveridge in the 'back seat' the landing was accomplished without incident. As the Phantom was in excellent condition, little work was anticipated for the conversation team other than repainting. However, for the American Air Museum, a decision was taken to display the Phantom in the US Navy colours it carried during service with VF-74 during the Vietnam operations. Geoff Ochs and Paul Rushen were in charge of identifying equipment added post 1972 and its removal. Fortunately, paint stripping the RAF scheme was undertaken by the AST Group as a demonstration whilst holding a customer conference at the Duxford Officers Mess during the spring of 1994. After re-spraying the most demanding task was applying the literally hundreds of small notices, mostly instructional, that were a feature of US Navy aircraft. This required many hours of intricate stencil work to effect, the task taking several months and not being completed until spring 1995. Meanwhile,

Geoff Ochs and Eric Perrott (who took over from Paul Rushen) also put solid filling in the tyres, refurbished and fitted a central fuel tank, speed brakes and radome. The final tasks involved modifying the ejection seats and the attaching of pylons and missiles with completion in the early months of 1996.

Crew	Two.
Engines	Two 17,900 lb (79.6kN) static thrust General Electric J79-GE-10 turbojets with afterburning.
Dimensions	Wing span 38 ft 4 in (11.68 m). Length 58 ft 2 in (17.73 m).
Weight	28,000 lb (12,701kg) empty. 44,600 lb (20,230 kg) loaded. 58,000 lb (26,308 kg) maximum.
Armament	Up to four AIM-9 Sidewinder and four AIM-7 Sparrow air-to-air missiles or up to 16,000 lb (7,257 kg) of bombs, rockets, missiles or fuel tanks on centreline and four wing pylons.
Performance	Maximum speed Mach 2.27 (about 1,500 mph, 2,414 kph). Cruise speed 575 mph (925 kph). Service ceiling 62,000 ft. Combat range 800 miles (1,287 km). Maximum range 2,500 miles (4,022 km).

Nose markings of the refurbished F-4J bearing the colours of VF-74. This was the first aircraft to be moved into the American Air Museum for ground positioning. (DUX 96-80-7 & DUX 96-80-9)

Fairchild Republic A-10A Thunderbolt II

Officially and unimaginatively called Thunderbolt II, the A-10 was more commonly known as the 'Warthog' through lack of aesthetic appeal. If not pleasing to behold the A-10 met the mission for which it was designed most admirably, that of armoured vehicle destruction. Heavily armed and configured for maximum survivability against ground fire, the type entered service with the USAF in 1976, a total of 731 being built. Major deployment was to the 81st Tactical Fighter Wing at Bentwaters and Woodbridge in the UK where 108 were on hand in six squadrons at peak inventory. A-10s were used to great effect in Desert Storm against Iraq using guided missiles, conventional bombs and the type's 30 mm multi-barrel cannon. Following the end of the Cold War the 81st Tactical Fighter Wing was inactivated after a forty year tenancy at Bentwaters.

One of the A-10s was presented on loan to the IWM, the aircraft selected being A-10A 77-0259 of the 511th Tactical Fighter Squadron. This 'Warthog' was built at the Hagerstown, Maryland plant and delivered to the USAAF storage center at Davis-Monthan AFB on 22 February 1979. On 26 March that year it was readied for movement to England and the 81st Tactical Fighter Wing, being assigned to the 510th Tactical Fighter Squadron on arrival at Bentwaters. The aircraft remained with the 81st TFW until its electronics and other equipment was deemed dated, the return flight to the USA commencing

Touchdown at Duxford, 6 February 1992. (DUX 92-3-8)

on 19 August 1981. On arrival 77-0259 was allotted for Air National Guard use, the 176th Tactical Fighter Squadron, 128th Tactical Fighter Wing at Truax Field, Wisconsin ANG operating it for seven years. Following major overhaul at McClellan AFB, California, in December 1988 the aircraft was sent to the 103rd Tactical Air Support Squadron, 111th Tactical Air Support Group of the Pennsylvania ANG for use in forward air control. However, in 1990 it was returned to the 176th Tactical Fighter Squadron and on 14 July 1990 arrived at Sculthorpe to participate in exercise 'Coronet Lariat'. It was then appropriated by the 3rd Air Force and exchanged for a 'time expired' A-10 which the ANG unit returned to the USA. The new assignment for 77-0259 was the 511th Tactical Fighter Squadron, which had recently been transferred from the 81st Tactical Fighter Wing to the 10th Tactical Reconnaissance Wing at Alconbury, albeit that its operational role was unchanged. The 511th was deployed in Saudi Arabia during the Gulf War of 1990-91 , but 77-0259 was transferred to a sister squadron, the 509th, remaining in the UK. After being flown to Duxford by Captain Mark Hedman on 6 February 1992, little conservation work was necessary apart from fully protecting the interior of the aircraft with long term preservative.

81ST TRAINING WING

Crew	One.
Engines	Two 9,065 lb (40.3 kN) thrust General Electric TF-34 turbofans.
Dimensions	Wing span 57 ft 6 in (17.53 m). Length 53 ft 4 in (16.26 m).
Weight	21,541 lb (9,771 kg) empty. 50,000 lb (22,680 kg) full load.
Armament	One GAU-8/A 30mm seven barrel cannon and 1,174 rounds. Up to 16,000 lb (7,258 kg) of ordnance comprising free-fall bombs, guided bombs, Maverick air-to-ground or Sidewinder air-to-air missiles on eight underwing and three underfuselage mounting points.
Performance	Maximum sea-level speed 439 mph (706 kph). Cruise speed 387 mph (623 kph). Service ceiling 30,500 ft (9,296 m). Combat range 576 miles (926 km).

Shortly after arrival at Duxford, February 1992. Not a pretty aircraft but it carried a lethal punch.
(DXP 92-77-6)

USAF armament personnel from Alconbury using a special lifting trolley to install a gun pack in '259'. The seven barrel, rapid fire weapon had been suitably inactivated beforehand. (DXP 92-23-2)

Lockheed U-2

The prefix letter U in USAF aircraft designations stands for Utility, but there was nothing utility about the U-2. This was simply a cover name for a very secret aircraft built to over-fly the USSR and gain information for the Central Intelligence Agency. Designed to operate at heights up to 75,000 feet where intercepting fighters of the time could not reach, the unarmed U-2 carried cameras and electronic gear. First flown in 1955, U-2s carried out reconnaissance of Soviet controlled territories unchecked until 1 May 1960 when the aircraft flown by Francis Powers was shot down by a surface-to-air missile. Thereafter U-2 operations were confined to the borders of the potential enemy's domain or areas where missile interception was unlikely, flying from bases in Turkey, Japan, Germany and Britain. U-2s provided the intelligence on ballistic missile build-up in Cuba in 1962 and the type has been used extensively in reconnaissance over the more recent Middle East and European trouble spots. U-2 presence in Britain became more open in the 1980s and the 95th Reconnaissance Squadron operated the type from Alconbury between October 1982 and September 1993.

The Duxford U-2 is one of only two examples this famous 'spyplane' on permanent exhibition in Europe (the other is in Norway). A U-2C, serial number 56-6692, it was originally a U-2A, the nineteenth built for the CIA

Now in single seat configuration the Duxford U-2 at one stage flew as a two-seat trainer 'White Bird' as a U-2CT. Similar to the above. Eric Schulzinger – Lockheed Martin Skunk Works

at Lockheed's small Bakersfield, California factory. Taken to the local airport and transported in a C-124 to the secret CIA airfield at Groom Lake, Nevada, it was first test flown in late October 1956. Disassembly followed and two weeks later the U-2 was flown by C-124 to Giebelstadt, Germany where CIA's Detachment A was based. For a year the aircraft was employed in clandestine operations over the western Soviet empire. Returned to the USA and after undergoing modifications, including extra fuel tankage, this U-2 went to CIA Detachment C at Atsugi, Japan in June 1958. From this location operations were conducted over the eastern USSR area.

The aircraft returned to the USA in September 1959 being based at Edwards North airfield for experimental and pilot training use. Hitherto operated by the CIA clandestine units, in December 1960 56-6692 was assigned to the USAF's 4080th Strategic Wing at Laughlin AFB, Texas where it served on detachment until the summer of 1962. With 1,653 hours flight time it was then converted from a U-2A to a U-2F model by Lockheed at Burbank, California entailing a new model engine and in-flight refuelling equipment. The aircraft was then returned to the CIA and after some time with its Detachment G at Edwards North airfield was sent to Detachment H at Taoyuan, Taiwan in June 1964. Under the auspices of the Republic of China Air Force operational flights were carried out over mainland China. Returned to the US in March 1965 for further equipment up-dates at Van Nuys, California it was back to Taiwan in May for nine more operational flights. This work completed 56-6692 was withdrawn to the CIA Edwards North before major modification at Van Nuys in February 1966. Between this date and April 1968 the aircraft oscillated between Edwards North and Van Nuys, being used to test new equipment and modifications. In April 1968 with over 3,500 hours flight time on the airframe 56-6692 was relinquished by the CIA but it continued its experimental role with the USAF at Edwards South being assigned to the 6515th Test Squadron. The aircraft remained at Edwards South until August 1974 when, with over 5,000 hours on the airframe, Lockheed carried out major overhaul, removing the in-flight refuelling reception installation and returning the U-2 to C model configuration. In its new guise the aircraft is believed to have been used in special equipment trials. During the autumn of 1995 the aircraft was converted to a trainer and assigned to the 100th Strategic Reconnaissance Wing at Davis-Monthan AFB in January 1976 and when that unit was inactivated in March, transferred to the 9th Strategic Reconnaissance Wing at Beale AFB, California. The final flight of 56-6692 was made on 28 December 1987 for a combined total of some 7,900 hours involving 11,330 individual flights.

Transported by air to RAF Alconbury on 22 February 1988 the aircraft was used for battle damage repair training. In September 1991 following IWM interest 56-6692 underwent restoration and return to single seat U-2C configuration by USAF volunteers with Lockheed technician help. Transported to Duxford by road the U-2 was officially received on 26 June 1992. For the ceremony Colonel Buzz Carpenter, Vice Commander of the Second Air Force, which controlled the active U-2 units in the USA, flew over to make the presentation. Art Schultz, Lockheed's Program Manager for the U-2 also came over

for the special event. Colonel Richard Riddick represented the Third Air Force which had permitted its staff to carry out the restoration work. As such an excellent refurbishment had been carried out on the U-2 at Alconbury only minor work was necessary by Duxford staff before the aircraft was suspended in a 20 degree climb attitude in the American Air Museum.

Crew	One.
Engine	One 17,000 lb (75.6 kN) static thrust Pratt & Whitney J75-P-13B turbojet.
Dimensions	Wing span 80 ft (24.4 m). Length 49 ft 7 in (15.16 m).
Weight	11,700 lb (5,307 kg) empty. 17,270 lb (7,833 kg) gross.
Armament	None.
Performance	Maximum speed 528 mph (849 kph) above 40,000 ft (12,192 m). Cruise speed 475 mph (764 kph). Operation ceiling 85,000 ft (25,925 m). Range 4,000 miles (6,436 km) with wing tanks. Endurance 10 hours.

One of the hardened aircraft shelters at Alconbury provided hangar cover for the U-2 while USAF volunteers returned it to single-seat configuration and gave a complete overhaul. When this photograph was taken early in 1992 a number of patches resulting from battle damage repair training were visible on the airframe. (DXP CN 92-28-1)

General Dynamics F-111

Economy in military and naval budgets during the early 1960s led to an advanced fighter design suitable for both the US Air Force and Navy. An innovative feature was 'variable geometry', a pivoting wing providing extended span for lift on take-off or slow landing on carriers and, swung to 72.5 degrees aft, configuration for supersonic capability. The result was an aircraft that was unacceptable as a fighter by both services. None were ordered by the US Navy and while the USAF bestowed the fighter designation F on those ordered, the 'One Eleven' was employed as a tactical bomber. Considerable trouble was experienced with the early F-111s' 'swing wings' when the aircraft entered service in 1967. Once development problems were overcome the F-111 proved an excellent low-level strike aircraft employing automatic ground-following radar. Although used on a limited scale during the South-East Asia war, the main force was deployed in the UK as the vehicle for NATO's tactical nuclear deterrent, later specialising in advanced laser-guided missiles. F-111E models equipped the 20th Tactical Fighter Wing at Upper Heyford from September 1970 to its disbandment in December 1993, and F-111Fs the 48th Tactical Fighter Wing at Lakenheath from March 1977 to December 1992. A small number of EF-111As with special electronic equipment for radar jamming were also on hand and at peak inventory 157 'One Elevens' were UK based. Lakenheath F-111s took part in the raid on Libyan terrorist locations 14 April 1986 and

A slow pass with everything down before the landing approach on 19 October 1993. (DUX CN 93-32-2)

both bases deployed their aircraft for operations in the Desert Storm action against Iraq. From an unhappy beginning, the F-111 proved to be an excellent strike aircraft. Production, terminated in 1976, ran to 562 aircraft.

The IWM's wish to enlarge the American aircraft collection resulted in the USAF Museum's loan of an F-111E when the type was withdrawn from service with the 20th Fighter Wing in 1993. Serial number 67-120, built in 1969 was delivered to the USAF on the last day of October. Its first year was spent with the 481st Tactical Fighter Squadron of the 27th Tactical Fighter Wing at Cannon AFB, New Mexico. The next twelve years were in operational training: from 24 November 1970 to 28 March 1978 with the 442nd Tactical Fighter Training Squadron at Nellis AFB, Nevada and from March 1978 to 22 October 1982 with the 57th Tactical Training Wing at McClean AFB, California. Refurbished, 67-120 was flown overseas to the UK and assigned to the 79th Tactical Fighter Squadron at Upper Heyford, later moving to the sister 77th Tactical Fighter Squadron, and participating in 19 combat missions during Desert Storm. The aircraft continued with the 77th until this squadron was due for inactivation in 1993, when it was taken over by the 55th Tactical Fighter Squadron. On retirement it had amassed a total of 5,300 flying hours. Flown into Duxford on 19 October 1993, concerns about sufficient runway length led to two portable arrester cables to ensure there was no over-run. A 7,500 feet runway is specified for a 24 ton F-111, 3,000 feet more than that available at Duxford. With arrester hook deployed pilot Captain Frank Rossi brought the aircraft in at 132 knots and caught the first cable. As one commentator observed the landing proved 'professionally uneventful'. The F-111 was then isolated while a team from British Aerospace, Filton, made the crew pod ejection mechanism safe, removing some 260 hazardous components. Little conservation work was necessary before the F-111E was placed in the American Air Museum. Its markings are representative of the aircraft's days with the 79th Tactical Fighter Squadron at Upper Heyford.

Bottom right: Switches everywhere. The pilots' compartment of the F-111E looking down and back from the left side.
(DUX CN 93-32-35 & DUX CN 93-32-33)

Above: The assigned aircraft of the 55th Tactical Fighter Squadron commander, the F-111E carried an Indian head insignia when delivered to Duxford. This was replaced by a tiger head representative of the 79th Tactical Fighter Squadron with which the aircraft first served at Upper Heyford. Ronald Wong rendered the new motif, photographed in a Duxford hangar with the artist.
(DUX CN 93-32-32 & DUX CN 95-1-30)

Crew	Two.
Engines	Two Pratt & Whitney TF-30-P-3 turbofans each of 18,550 lb (82.5 kN) static thrust with afterburning.
Dimensions	Wing span spread 63 ft (19.2 m). Wing span swept 31 ft 11½ in (9.74 m). Length 73 ft 6 in (22.4 m).
Weight	45,700 lb (20,730 kg) empty. 92,500 lb (41,960 kg) full load.
Armament	Two 750 lb (340 kg) nuclear or conventional bombs or 20 mm multi-barrel cannon in internal bay and up to 25,000 lb (11,340 kg) of bombs, rockets, missiles or fuel tanks on four underwing pylons.
Performance	Maximum sea-level speed, Mach 1.2 about 912 mph, (1,467 kph). Maximum speed at altitude, Mach 2.5 about 1,650 mph (2,655 kph). Service ceiling 66,000 ft (20,117 m). Combat range on internal fuel 2,925 miles (4,700 km).

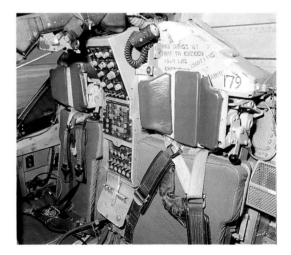

Schweizer TG-3A

Following the successful use of glider-borne infantry by the Germans in their 1940 campaigns, the US Army showed interest in developing a similar capability. A two-seat dual-control glider was required for training pilots and to meet this objective military versions of popular sailplanes were ordered in 1941. One of these was based on a Schweizer design, three prototypes being procured under the designation XTG-3. A major difference between the civilian and the military models was the latter's use of wood instead of aluminium for the basic structure. Only 111 TG-3As were made as less expensive basic gliders were made from engineless versions of Aeronca, Taylorcraft and Piper light aircraft, which also had flight characteristics more akin to the Waco assault gliders to which student pilots progressed.

The Duxford TG-3A, serial number 42-52988, was offered to Duxford by Chris Manley of Mojave, California, one of the Founding Members of the American Air Museum in Britain. Not registered for civilian flight – as N66630 – until 1963, its earlier history is obscure, although the glider was apparently in storage for many years. Shipped from California in spring 1996, conservation work entailed reassembly and minor repairs plus a re-spray in USAAF training colours. Suspension fittings were installed and the TG-3A at under a ton became the lightest of the eight aircraft hung from the American Air Museum roof.

Crew	Two.
Dimensions	Wing span 54 ft (16.5 m). Length 27 ft 7 in (8.4 m).
Weight	820 lb (327 kg) empty. 1,200 lb (544 kg) gross.
Performance	Maximum speed towed or free 100 mph (160 kph).

Lifting the TG-3A to the ceiling. At under 800 lb, it is the lightest of all the suspended aircraft in the American Air Museum. (DUX CN 96-1-1015)

Boeing-Stearman PT-17

The Stearman biplane, first ordered as a primary trainer for the US Army in 1931, appeared under the designations PT-9, PT-13, PT-17, PT-18 and PT-27 as the design was developed and re-engined over the next decade. Under the designation N2S the Stearman also served the US Navy and the PT-27s were supplied to the Royal Canadian Air Force. In its various forms more than six thousand of these hardy, dependable aircraft were built making the Stearman the most numerous of all American biplanes. PT-17s used Continental radial engines and 3,519 were built. In addition to being the main type on which US pilots commenced training during the Second World War, Stearmans were also loaned to China and Central and South American countries.

The Duxford example, ex-USAAF serial 41-8169, found it way to Canada having, like many Stearmans, been sold for commercial usage during the early post-war years. The type's robust construction and inherent stability made it popular with agricultural contracting services, notably for crop spraying and dusting. Evergreen Aviation Services used 41-8169, Canadian registration CF-EQS, for some years, the front cockpit being modified to take a hopper and dispenser for agricultural materials. Damage and deterioration caused the biplane to be grounded and later acquired by the IWM.

Shipped to the UK in the mid 1980s the parts were put into storage at Duxford. With the Stearman scheduled for the American Air Museum, it was removed from storage in spring of 1993. Conservation officer Chris Knapp carried out a thorough inspection of the components and found that much of the wood in airframe and wings was rotten. After estimating the work entailed, and given that Stearmans were relatively common, a decision was made that renovation investment was not justified. The parts were returned to storage to await a further decision on the fate of 41-8169. However, wishing to include this important type in the American Air Museum, and after being unable to find another PT-17 for static display, discussions with Eastern Stearman Ltd resulted in a decision to have 41-8169 rebuilt. This Swanton Morley based firm, specialised in the maintenance and overhaul of the many privately operated Stearmans in Europe, completed the work under contract at their premises, returning the components to Duxford in February 1997 where the aircraft was re-assembled. As much of 41-8169 was beyond repair components were obtained from another Stearman, AAF serial 42-17786, making the rebuilt aircraft a composite. Prior to suspending in the new building a wartime USAAF paint scheme was applied. Borley Brothers of Teversham carried out the transfer and suspension of the Stearman in the new building, a somewhat difficult task as other aircraft were already positioned on the floor area.

Airborne but static. (DUX 97-1-161)

Crew	Two.
Engine	One 220 hp (164 kW) Continental R-670 seven-cylinder radial.
Dimensions	Wing span 32 ft 2 in (9.8 m). Length 25 ft (7.6 m).
Weight	1,931 lb (876 kg) empty. 2,635 lb (1,195 kg) loaded.
Performance	Maximum speed 124 mph (200 kph). Cruising speed 106 mph (171 kph). Service ceiling 11,200 ft (3,416 m). Range 505 miles (813 km).

North American AT-6D Texan

A composite built up specially for the Museum, most of the Texan originated as a Canadian built AT-16 which served with the RCAF and later the RNAF. (DUX 96-1-934)

Built as an AT-16ND by Noorduyn Aviation of Montreal under a US financed contract, the aircraft was constructor number 14-718 and USAAF serial 42-12471. Allotted to the RAF under Lend/Lease as Harvard IIB, serial FE984, it was diverted to the RCAF on leaving the factory and served at No 2 Flying Instructor School (Canada). Other service history is obscure but the aircraft eventually went to the Royal Netherlands Air Force where its identity was B-168. The Aircraft Restoration Company were responsible for the rebuild and finish of the Texan for the IWM.

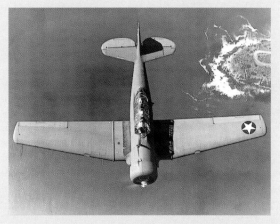

Classic plan view of an early USAAF AT-6 Texan. *USAAF*

The best known and most prolific advanced trainer of the Second World War originated as North American model NA-19 in 1935 and gathered many designations as the design was developed. More than 19,000 were built and served many air forces, with production also undertaken in Canada and Australia. RAF versions were named Harvard, the batch ordered in 1938 being one of the first post-First World War British purchases from an American manufacturer. Wartime production concentrated on the AT-6D model of which 4,388 were built with those in USAAF service known as Texans. Apart from becoming the main Allied advanced trainer of the Second World War, the AT-6D served operationally in Korea for tactical air control and had similar usage by the RAF in Malaya and Kenya during the 1950s. Texans served both the USAAF and USAF in the UK, 1944 to 1950 for communications purposes.

The AT-6D suspended in the American Air Museum was obtained in April 1996 from John Romain's The Aircraft Restoration Co. Ltd, a private concern based at Duxford. This is a composite, the fuselage and the majority of parts coming from a former Royal Netherlands Air Force aircraft held at Duxford for spares since September 1989.

Crew	Two.
Engine	One 600 hp (447 kW) Pratt & Whitney R-1340 radial.
Dimensions	Wing span 42 ft (12.80 m). Length 29 ft (8.84 m).
Weight	4,271 lb (1,937 kg) empty. 5,617 lb (2,548 kg) loaded.
Armament	Two fixed 0.30 machine guns. Provision for one 0.30 in machine gun on flexible mount in the cockpit. Bomb racks under wings for various practice bombs.
Performance	Maximum speed 208 mph (335 kph). Service ceiling 21,500 ft (6,557 m). Range 750 miles (1,206 km).

SPAD S.XIII

The sole representative of American military aviation from the First World War, the suspended Spad S-13 is actually a replica, albeit having flown for display purposes. In the 1980s Duxford received a genuine Spad VII which the IWM had on loan from M Louis Blériot and was displayed in one of the hangars for several years. Planning centred on using this aircraft in the American Air Museum but unfortunately the loan was suddenly terminated in 1995 when the owner decided to return the Spad to France and make it airworthy. Finding another genuine Spad or alternative First World War type was highly unlikely. However, a replica Spad was located on static display at the Fleet Air Arm Museum, Yeovilton and IWM were able to secure this for the American Air Museum. Made in Germany during the 1960s it was later operated by the Thorpe Park Flying Circus of Surrey as G-BFYO. Some worrying flight characteristics led to permanent grounding in 1982 and purchase by the Fleet Air Arm Museum four years later. Brought to Duxford by road in 1997 the Spad was painted under contract in the colours of the 94th Pursuit Squadron aircraft flown by Captain Edward Rickenbacker, the top scoring American fighter ace with 26 victories achieved flying on the Western Front. All but two of the 18 operational pursuit squadrons of the American Expeditionary Force in France were equipped with Spads. Having no suitable indigenous fighter aircraft on entering hostilities, in March 1918 the US Government made purchases of Spads from the French and British production of the type, eventually amounting to 893 machines.

Awaiting movement into the American Air Museum in 1996. The markings are as carried on Eddie Rickenbacker's 1918 Spad. (DUX 96-84-25 & DUX 96-84-36)

Crew	One.
Engine	One 235 hp (175 kW) Hispano-Suiza water cooled V8.
Dimensions	Wing span 26 ft 4 in (8.05 m). Length 20 ft 4 in (6.22 m).
Weight	1,255 lb (569 kg) empty. 1,811 lb (821 kg) gross.
Armament	Two .303 in. Vickers or .300 in Marlin machine guns.
Performance	Maximum speed 138 mph (222 kph). Service ceiling 22,300 ft (6,801 m).

The Spad represents the United States involvement in First World War military aviation. (DUX 97-1-616)

North American F-86A Sabre

The USAF's first swept-wing jet fighter, the Sabre entered squadron service in 1949. The outbreak of the Korean War the following year found F-86s deployed to counter the surprising Soviet MiG-15 which also featured a swept wing. The F-86 being heavier than the MiG-15 and less manoeuvrable was initially at a disadvantage, but the American pilots developed tactics which eventually gave them air superiority. These were the first jet versus jet battles of air warfare. Total Sabre production between 1947 and 1955 ran to 4,490, the type appearing in several versions to meet air defence and ground support missions. Because of its performance advance over other fighters in the air forces of US aligned nations the Sabre had widespread use during the 1950s. The first Sabres in Europe, F-86As of the 81st Fighter Interceptor Wing, arrived at Shepherds Grove, Suffolk in August 1951 to provide air defence for USAF bomber bases. Later Sabre models equipped several USAF wings based on the Continent supporting the NATO mission.

Such a military aviation milestone as the Sabre was an obvious candidate for the American Air Museum. There was little opportunity to obtain one for static display as with so many vintage fighter types remaining examples are kept airworthy. During 1994 the IWM came to a tentative arrangement with Planes of Fame Museum, Chino, California to exchange an ex-RAF Meteor F.4 for an F-86A.

F-86As of the 4th Fighter Interceptor Wing scramble from a Korean airfield. *US National Archive*

The deal included restoration of the aircraft by the respective parties before exchange and was finalised in 1996. Much of the refurbishment of the Meteor was carried out under contract by the Aircraft Restoration Company, although the wings were reworked by ex-IWM employee Eddie West on contract, and the rear fuselage and tail surfaces by Phil Earthey, also on contract. The Sabre arrived crated at Duxford on 26 June 1997. When unpacked the aircraft proved to be a considerable disappointment in terms of completeness and standard of restoration. A considerable number of items were missing and the wing proved to be of a later broad chord type as used on F-86F models. Representations were made to Planes of Fame and a settlement involving an offset agreement for a P-47 propeller and later supply of F-86 parts was agreed. Only cosmetic work could be done on the Sabre before the 1 August opening of the American Air Museum. The fuselage and wings were manoeuvred separately through the emergency double doors in the glass wall that fronts the building and the aircraft was reassembled in position in the building.

Investigation of the history of this F-86A, serial number 48-0242, found that it was built at Inglewood, California and completed on 7 April 1949. After modifications the Sabre was accepted by the USAF on 7 July 1949 and a week later delivered to the 4th Fighter Group at Langley Field, Virginia. This was the group formed from the RAF Eagle Squadrons during the Second World War. Service with this unit was brief as sometime later in the year the Sabre was involved in an accident, probably a crash-landing. Damage was sufficiently bad for the aircraft to be written off on 5 December 1949. The fuselage was then used on a USAF mobile recruiting vehicle. Sold by the US government in the 1970s, the remains were lodged at Chino with Planes of Fame for many years.

The fuselage is withdrawn from a transport container, 26 June 1997. (DUX 97-1-481)

As all major aircraft exhibits were in place, getting the F-86 to its planned position required a great deal of manoeuvring with only inches to spare at some places. The muscle power of (left to right) Jim Morgan, Doug Rigden and Martin Barnes being applied to get the fuselage under the B-29's wing. (DUX 97-1-497)

Reassembled in position and now the object of acclaim by early visitors to the newly opened museum. (DUX 97-1-772)

Crew	One.
Engine	One General Electric J47-GE-13 turbojet of 5,200 lb (23.1 kN) thrust or 6,000 lb (26.7 kN) with water injection.
Dimensions	Wing span 37 ft 1 in (11.3m). Length 36 ft 7 in (11.2 m).
Weight	10,495 lb (4,760 kg) empty. 16,357 lb (7,430 kg) loaded.
Armament	Six 0.50 in Colt-Browning machine guns.
Performance	Maximum speed 675 mph (1,086 kph). Service ceiling 48,300 ft (14,731 m). Combat range with drop tanks 1,270 miles (2,043 km).

Bell UH-1H Iroquois

The wish to have some helicopter representation in the American Air Museum led to IWM approaches securing the gift of a UH-1H from the US Army. Designed principally for casualty evacuation the type was widely used throughout the Vietnam war for combat zone troop transportation. Use of the UH-1's official name was limited as a spoken distortion of its designation – originally HU-1 – soon resulted in the universally popular 'Huey'. Built under licence in Italy, Japan and Taiwan and used by several nations some 12,000 UH-1 and variants were built over twenty years.

IWM's request to US authorities in November 1996, resulted in the gift of a surplus UH-1H the following January. US Army Troop Command Europe supplied the Huey which was meticulously prepared by volunteer staff at Coleman Barracks, Mannheim. The aircraft had been in Germany since 1988 when it was assigned to V Corps, 158th Aviation Regiment. An RAF Hercules delivered the aircraft, serial number 72-21605, to Duxford on 15 July 1997. Transfer was delayed by a certain amount of military bureaucracy. The helicopter then had to be manhandled through one of the double doors in the glass wall with both doors and frame hinged back to give a 9 by 16 feet opening. Even then the rotor had to be removed to reduce overall height and once inside, to reach the display position, it was necessary to jack up the B-25 so that the Huey could be moved under the wing.

Last aircraft to go into the building – late in the afternoon of arrival at Duxford – there was only just room to pass through the emergency door in the glass wall. (DUX 97-1-592)

The Iroquois saw very wide service, especially in Vietnam. Illustrated is a UH-1E of the US Marine Corps. *Bell*

Crew	Two.
Engine	One 1,100 hp (820 kW) Lycoming T53-L-11 turboshaft.
Dimensions	Rotor diameter 48 ft (13.4 m). Fuselage length 41 ft 7½ in (12.7 m).
Weight	4,369 lb (1,982 kg) empty. 8,500 lb (3,856 kg) maximum.
Armament	None.
Performance	Maximum speed 138 mph (222 kph). Cruising speed 126 mph (202 kph). Hovering ceiling 12,500 ft (3,812 m). Range 253 miles (407 km).

Consolidated B-24 Liberator

From the earliest days of the move to establish the USAAF collection at Duxford a B-24 Liberator was identified as a 'must'. Not only was this running mate with the B-17 Fortress in the Eighth Air Force's daylight strategic bombing campaign, its worldwide use in several roles saw it probably contributing more to Allied victory than any other aircraft type. Designed as a heavy bomber it also served as a long range transport and was particularly successfully for oceanic patrol in anti-submarine work. Liberators served with Bomber, Transport and Coastal Commands of the RAF and Commonwealth air forces, the US Navy also used the type for oceanic patrol. Built in larger numbers than any other US aircraft of the Second World War, five production sources delivered 19,256, the Ford Motor Company applying its automobile mass production techniques to alone complete 6,792 at its giant Willow Run facility and 1,893 more in the form of knockdown assemblies sent to other plants. The largest single concentration of Liberators was in the UK during June 1944 when some 1,500 were present, most in 78 Eighth

Air Force squadrons. There were also 60 B-24 squadrons with the Fifteenth Air Force in Italy. Undoubtedly the most famous American bomber operation of the war, was the low-level bombing of the Ploesti oil refineries in Roumania, flown by 179 B-24s, 56 of which were lost.

At the time the Duxford USAAF Collection was begun few Liberators still existed, the most notable source being India where late production Liberators used by the RAF in the closing months of the war with Japan were taken over by the Indian Air Force and flown for some twenty years. One of these was purchased by US collector Dave Tallichet, and flown to Duxford for overhaul and repainting in October 1973. It was hoped the owner could be persuaded to keep the aircraft at Duxford but after a 23 month stay it was flown to the US,

The airworthy David Tallichet Liberator which remained at Duxford for nearly two years. DAS members worked on the aircraft and Gerry Collins painted it to represent a 389th Bomb Group B-24J named *Delectable Doris*. *Steve Gotts*

ROOTIN' TOOTIN' RAT'ILIN' BANG was the slogan found on the B-24D nose section. (DXP 95-43-6)

having gathered the name *Delectable Doris* and a paint scheme representative of the 389th Bomb Group. IWM made enquiries about any remaining Liberators in India through the London embassy but in the meantime British aviation collector-dealer Doug Arnold had managed to find, arrange disassembly and air transport, of another Indian Liberator albeit a grounded example. This was stored at Blackbushe and offered for sale. The Confederate Air Force carried out a survey and concluded that making the aircraft airworthy was not an economical proposition. Then, in 1983, the 8th Air Force Memorial Museum Foundation made enquiries on behalf of the IWM with a view to purchasing the aircraft to rebuild for static display. However, before this endeavour progressed very far Bob Collings, a young American computer millionaire, paid Arnold's asking price and shipped the Liberator to the USA. There the aircraft was restored to superb flying condition at great expense and under the auspices of the Collings Foundation became a frequent star turn at air displays in the 1990s.

Undaunted, the IWM then turned its attention to acquiring one of the four B-24s owned by the USAF Museum located at different USAF installations. Despite the cause being a tribute of US military aviation achievement there was obvious need of high-level military and political support to overcome reluctance to allow a B-24 to leave the USA. As the American Air Museum in Britain campaign gathered pace and the building became a reality so some very influential contacts were made. Ford backed the venture with $500,000 and discussions with

The wreckage as received at Duxford turned out to be from two different model Liberators. The nose part is possibly from B-24D 41-11874 and the cockpit section was definitely taken from B-24J 42-51457. Allegedly, these sections were on an MGM film lot in Hollywood before acquisition by NASM. (DUX 96-5-43)

Andy Robinson (left) and Ralph Warren reconstructing the B-24 nose framing. All glazing was missing and had to be specially manufactured. Detail reveals the nose to be from a very early B-24D. (DUX 97-1-473)

Work on the interior which would hold a visual display unit for screening the documentary narrated by Charlton Heston. (DUX 97-12-10)

Designated EZB-24M, the Liberator's last flying use was on ice research flights for which it had special monitoring equipment.

Dismantling the aircraft at Lackland AFB was carried out by the three man Duxford team with assistance of World Wide Aircraft Recovery, a recommended US company which had the necessary lifting and transport equipment. The task was completed within two weeks.

the USAF Museum centred on a possible exchange of an aircraft type they required for a B-24. The most likely candidate was a B-24M that had reposed outdoors at Lackland AFB, San Antonio, Texas. In May 1995 David Lee, Duxford's Deputy Director, was taken to Lackland by US Board member Marshall Cloyd to survey the Liberator, before going on to the Lone Star Flight Museum, Galve-

ston to discuss dismantling and transportation of the aircraft. Externally well preserved, many modifications had been made to the Liberator and it would obviously take much work to restore to a wartime configuration. As a result of this visit a formal request for the loan of this aircraft, sponsored by Ford , was submitted to the USAF.

Meanwhile Edward Inman had obtained two sections of a B-24 nose which the National Air and Space Museum in Washington had in store and these were shipped to the UK late in 1995. Determined to see some representation of this famous aircraft in the American Air Museum, the intention was to refurbish and display this nose until a complete aircraft was available. On examination at Duxford the two sections of nose were found to be both badly corroded, gutted of most fixtures and from two different B-24s! In fact, the nose section was from an early B-24D used for training and the cockpit section from a

B-24J. Conservation officer Andy Robinson had the unenviable task of making this presentable in just 12 months. That he and his helpers managed to turn a marginal piece of corroded structure into a first-rate exhibit in less than ten months was a remarkable achievement. The finished piece was appropriately painted as *Fighting Sam*, with an aggressive Uncle Sam cartooned brandishing his fists as marked on an actual B-24D that flew with the 389th Bomb Group at Hethel.

There were still high hopes of obtaining the Lackland B-24, with a proposal that the aircraft be on loan for 12 years in return for a fibreglass replica being made to take its place. The procurement of a replica was subject to considerable difficulties in relation to price, longevity, structural safety and future liabilities. However, the USAF Museum were more interested in an exchange and by the winter of 1997-98 discussions had centred on the IWM providing a Spitfire VB. This suggestion had been made at an earlier date but the IWM did not have a Spitfire available for trade. Fortunately at this juncture a Spitfire V, put up for sale in Australia, was secured for the IWM by Aero Vintage Ltd for approximately £340,000. The exchange was a much simpler arrangement; it also had the advantage that the B-24 would belong to the IWM. The deal, subject to the Chief of Staff of the USAF giving approval, was forthcoming in November 1998 when a formal agreement between the two parties was signed. Part of the agreement was that the Spitfire be refurbished partly by the IWM at Duxford and partly by Aero Vintage and painted to represent one used by a US Twelfth Air Force unit. The provision of a fibreglass replica for Lackland became the responsibility of the US Air Force Museum.

In May 1999 a Duxford Conservation team, Chris Knapp, Keith Trigg and Harmon King, flew out to Lackland to help and oversee the disassembly work of contractors World Wide Aircraft Recovery who had been recommended for the task. First parts of the B-24 to arrive at Duxford came by C-130 on 3 June and included engines, propellers, wheels and bomb doors. The main sections were flown from Kelly AFB to Mildenhall in a C-5 Galaxy on 28 June and transported to Duxford by road the same day.

Built as a B-24M-25-FO, serial number 44-51228, at Willow Run, Michigan early in 1945, the aircraft had spent most of its usage in ice research redesignated as an EZB-24M. For this purpose special equipment was installed in a much modified nose. When retired in 1956 it was believed to be the last Liberator operated by the USAF. It had then spent the next 43 years on display at Lackland AFB's parade ground.

The mainplane arrives at Duxford, wheel wells and turbo-superchargers predominant. (DX 99-44-31)

Crew	Ten.
Engines	Four 1,200 hp (895 kW) Pratt & Whitney R-1820 radials with turbochargers.
Dimensions	Wing span 110 ft (33.5 m). Length 66 ft 4 in (20.25 m).
Weight	34,000 lb (15,422 kg) empty. 60,000 lb (27,216 kg) maximum load.
Armament	Ten 0.50 in calibre machine guns. Maximum 8000 lb (3,628 kg) bombs in bay. Maximum load including external racks 12,800 lb (5,806 kg).
Performance	Top speed 303 mph (488 kph) at 25,000 ft (7,625 m). Cruising speed 216 mph (347 kph). Service ceiling 28,000 ft (8,540 m). Combat range with 5,000 lb (2,268 kg) bombs, 2,700 miles (4,344 km).

Lockheed SR-71A 'Blackbird'

The 'Blackbird' outside a Mildenhall 'barn' hangar on 6 December 1984. Fully fuel loaded these aircraft grossed over 72 short tons. *Bob Archer*

A high altitude reconnaissance aircraft developed from the A-12 design and subject to much secrecy in the early years of its existence. For a quarter of a century the SR-71A was claimed to be the highest flying and fastest aircraft in operational military service. Of the 32 aircraft built, 29 were SR-71As for operational employment, two were SR-71B dual control trainers, and one an SR-71C a hybrid dual-control trainer built to replace the loss of a standard trainer model. The SR-71A first entered service in May 1966 and the type was concentrated in the 9th Strategic Reconnaissance Wing based at Beale AFB, California. For overseas employment the SR-71As were operated by detachments of the 9th SRW, notably Detachment 1 at Kadena AB, Okinawa for Far East cover, and Detachment 4 at RAF Mildenhall for Europe and the Middle East. The Mildenhall detachment was established in 1989 and usually one, later two, of these aircraft occupied specially built hangars known as 'barns' on this airfield. Although the SR-71A had a maximum speed in excess of Mach 3 and could operate at altitudes up to 85,000 feet, by the mid-1980s satellites could more economically carry out the reconnaissance intelligence mission. Most SR-71As were withdrawn from service early in 1990 and put in storage. Because of its overall heat absorbing black finish the SR-71A was popularly known as the Blackbird.

SR-71A serial 64-17962 made its first flight on 29 April 1966 with Lockheed test crew William Weaver and Steven Belgau. Delivered to Beale AFB on 24 May 1966 this was to be the aircraft's main base for the next 24 years. In the hands of Robert Helt and Larry Elliott, 64-17962 reached a height of 85,068 feet setting a world altitude record on 28 July 1976. The aircraft was first deployed to RAF Mildenhall on 6 September 1976, remaining twelve days. There were further deployments with Detachment 4 at Mildenhall during the 1980s. However, 64-17962 was serving with Detachment 1 at Kadena when as the last SR-71A to use that base it returned to Beale on 21 January 1990. Retired to Lockheed's storage facility at Palmdale, California the aircraft remained in storage for 11 years until presented to the Imperial War Museum for permanent exhibition, becoming the only example of this type outside the United States. World Aircraft Recovery of Omaha, Nebraska dismantled and arranged for the transportation of the 'Blackbird' from Palmdale to Houston. Broken down into six main parts – forward and aft fuselage, right and left nacelle and two out wing panels – the aircraft arrived at Houston docks on 27 February 200. After re-assembly at Duxford the SR-71 was made available for a Press Day on 11 April. Positioning within the American Air Museum is scheduled to be completed by July 2002.

Crew	Two.
Engines	2 Pratt & Whitney J-58 turbojets of 32,500 lb (144.5 kN) thrust per engine.
Dimensions	Wing span 55 ft 7 ins (16.94 m). Length 107 ft 5 ins (32.74 m).
Weight	60,000 lb empty (27,216 kg). 170,000 lb air refuelled loaded (77,272 kg).
Performance	Top speed Mach 3.2 (2,214 mph) (3,542 km/h). Service ceiling 85,000 ft (25,914 m). Combat range 2,981 miles (4,769 km).

Instantly recognisable from any angle, the SR-71 has been the subject of many stunning photo-shoots.
Eric Schulzinger – Lockheed Aeronautical Systems

Opposite page:
The official handover of the SR-71 64-17962, took place at Duxford in a ceremony on 14th June 2001. The Blackbird is officially on loan from the USAF Museum at Dayton, Ohio. General Joseph W Ralston USAF, Supreme Allied Commander Europe (inset), performed the handover at what was claimed to be the largest ever gathering of former SR-71 aircrew.
Both Duncan Cubitt – FlyPast Magazine

Republic F-105D Thunderchief

Developed from the outset for a tactical mission, the F-105 was the first supersonic fighter-bomber to incorporate an internal weapons bay. The prototype of 1955 was followed by 75 F-105Bs and the main production model, the F-105D first flew on 9 June 1959. A total of 610 F-105Ds were built and seven USAF tactical fighter wings were eventually equipped with this model, two based in Germany. The F-105 was employed extensively in combat operations during the South East Asia conflict operating from bases in South Vietnam and Thailand. During the period 1965-1968 some 75 per cent of air strikes against North Vietnam were carried out Thunderchiefs although losses were high, amounting to half the total production of the type. It was estimated that an F-105 pilot had only a 75 per cent chance of surviving a 100 missions over North Vietnam. Most losses were to anti-aircraft ground fire. The type was noted for its load carrying ability and the robust construction that enabled it to survive substantial battle damage. The total production of all F-105 models amounted to 833 and the last aircraft was retired from USAF service in July 1980.

The F-105D selected for presentation to the Imperial War Museum as of 30 November 1997 has a notable history. Accepted by the USAF from Republic's Farmingdale plant on 14 March 1961, F-105D serial 59-1822 was flown to Nellis AFB, Nevada two days later with assignment to the 4520 Combat Crew Training Wing. The aircraft remained with the 4520 CCTW until the summer of 1963 when, on 22 July, it was returned to Farmingdale for update modifications and overhaul. On 8 October 1963 59-1822 was assigned to the 355th Tactical Fighter Wing at George AFB, California and, apart from depot overhaul, remained with this unit until the end of 1965. In January '65 it moved with the 355th TFW to McConnell AFB, Kansas and on 12 July was deployed with the wing's 357th Tactical Fighter Squadron to Korat AB, Thailand for combat operations. On return from SEA 59-1822 went for overhaul at McClellan AFB California in January 1966 and then back to McConnell on 3 March 1966 where it joined the 23rd TFW. Apart from transfers for upgrades and depot maintenance, this Thunderchief was operated by the 23rd TFW until early June the following year.

A trio of F-105Ds with centre-line and underwing long range tanks. *Republic*

Major Don Kutyna had a Polish national shield painted on both sides of the nose and the nickname The Polish Glider on both wing roots. RE on the tail was the 44th TFS code. *D Kutyna*

Flown out to Japan where it was held by the 6441st TFW as of 13 June 1967 before being transferred to the 18th TFW at Kadena AB, Okinawa ten days later. Initially assigned to the wing's 12th TFS, apart from a detachment to Osan, Korea, 59-1822 remained at Kadena for eleven months. A requirement for reinforcements in the SEA combat zone saw 59-1822 leave Okinawa on 23 May 1968 and two days join the 388th TFW at Korat AB, Thailand. This second spell of operational employment lasted until September. On at least two occasions 59-1822 sustained light battle damage. The first, on 13 July, was an inch hole in the top and bottom of the right wing tip and a 2 inch hole in the right outboard pylon. Further battle damage occurred on or about 1 September.

Returned to the USA in late September 1968 the aircraft was put into storage at McClellan on 21 October and later underwent a major overhaul. During 1969 F-105D 59-1822 was sent out to SEA for a third combat employment. This time it joined the 355th TFW, which had been its first-line assignment back in 1963. The 355th was based at Takhli AB, Thailand and 59-1822 served with the wing's 44th TFS and its regular pilot, Major Donald Kutyna named it *The Polish Glider*, acknowledging his Polish ancestry. Withdrawn for maintenance by Air Asia at Tainan Airport, Taiwan during June and July 1970, the aircraft continued with the 355th TFW until 24 October 1970 when it was prepared for transfer, being returned to the 23rd TFW at McConnell on the 27th of that month to become classified as flyable storage.

On 20 February 1971 F-105D left USAF service, being allotted to the Air National Guard. For the next ten years 59-1822 served with the 192nd Tactical Fighter Group at Byrd Field, Richmond, Virginia. During this time it was operated by the 149th TFS and for a period carried the name Superhog with an appropriate warthog motif. Towards the end of its time with the 192nd TFG 59-1822 was briefly loaned to the 116th TFW at Dobbins AFB, Georgia for use as a maintenance trainer. When finally retired the aircraft had a total of 3,513.1 flying hours on arrival at Davis-Monthan AFB, Arizona for storage. After twenty years at Davis-Monthan 59-1822, one of only a half dozen still surviving at this depot, was shipped to the UK for permanent preservation.

Crew	One.
Engine	One Pratt & Whitney J75-P-19W turbojet rated 17,200 lb (76.5 kN) static thrust.
Dimensions	Span 34 ft 11 in (10.65 m). Length 64 ft 3 in (19.58 m).
Weight	Empty 27,500 lb(12,485 kg). Maximum loaded 52,546 lb (23,855. 88 kg).
Armament	One M-61 20 mm multi-barrel rotary cannon. Maximum ordnance load 13,000 lb (5,902 kg).
Performance	Top speed 1,390 mph (Mach 2.1) (2,237.9 km/h). Cruise speed 778 mph (1,244.8 km/m). Service ceiling 50,000 ft (15,244 m). Combat range 2,208 miles (2,560 km).

F-105D 59-1822 photographed when serving with the 44th TFS, 355th TFW at Takhli Air Base in 1970.

McDonnell-Douglas F-15A Eagle

F-15A 76-0020 photographed at Alconbury on 14 September 1978 when serving with the 525th TFS, 36th TFW at Bitburg. *M France via G Pennick*

Designed as an air superiority interceptor, the F-15 was at the time of its introduction into service the most sophisticated and expensive fighter type in the world, but with a justifying performance. The first F-15A equipped unit deployed in Europe, to afford NATO defence against the high performance Soviet interceptors, was the 525th Tactical Fighter Squadron. This unit joined the 36th Tactical Fighter Wing at Bitburg, Germany in April 1977. F-15As were withdrawn from USAFE in November 1981, being replaced by the improved F-15C and D models. A total of 384 F-15A models were built.

The F-15A acquired by the Imperial War Museum, serial 76-0020, was built in 1976 and delivered to the 36th TFW at Bitburg AB, Germany in July 1977. It served with the 36th for approximately four years, returning to the USA in August 1981 for overhaul at Warner Robins Air Logistics Area, Robins AFB, Georgia. During its time with the 36th TFW, 76-0020 is known to have visited USAF bases in the UK. In December 1981 76-0020 was assigned to the 60th TFS of the 33rd TFW at Eglin AFB, Florida.

The next assignment recorded in available records was with the 5th Fighter Interceptor Squadron at Minot AFB, North Dakota. In January 1988 the aircraft was passed from service with regular USAF units to the Air National Guard and taken on strength by the 101st FIS, 102nd Fighter Interceptor Wing at Otis AFB, Massachusetts. This assignment was terminated in February 1992

and on 25 October 1993 the aircraft is recorded as being placed in storage at Davis-Monthan AFB, Arizona. Later F-15C and D models equip the 48th TFW at Lakenheath, the only major USAF combat organisation remaining in the UK following the end of the 'Cold War'.

Crew	One.
Engines	Two Pratt & Whitney F100-PW-100 turbofans rated at 25,000 lb (111.2 kN) static thrust each.
Dimensions	Span 42 ft 9¾in (13.04 m). Length 63 ft 9in (19.43m).
Weight	Loaded 56,000 lb.
Armament	One M-61A1 Vulcan cannon, four AIM-7 Sparrow and four AIM-9 Sidewinder missiles. Up to 15,000 lb (6,818.1 kg) external ordnance.
Performance	Top speed 1,600 mph (2,580 km/h). Service ceiling 65,000 ft (19,817m). Combat range 3,450 miles (5520 km).

Two of the latest arrivals, seen *in situ* at Duxford during Spring 2001 and awaiting full assembly and restoration. The F-105 will find its place in the American Air Museum in the foreseeable future, whilst the F-15 is perhaps unlikely to be brought into the museum in the short term. *Both Duncan Cubitt, Key Publishing*

Opposite page: The cruise missile launch trailer held four BGM-109G missiles in the rear compartment and control equipment in the forward section. Four of these trailers and two mobile control vehicles comprised an operational flight. The TEL in the American Air Museum was delivered to Duxford in October 1992. (DXP 94-15)

Supporting Exhibits

In addition to the aircraft, several pieces of associated air power hardware are displayed in the Museum, most notably the missiles that were to dominate both offensive and defensive action in the later stages of the century.

General Dynamics BGM-109G Tomahawk & TEL trailer

A so-called cruise missile, the Tomahawk, developed by General Dynamics and powered by a lightweight turbo-fan engine, was first deployed in Europe in November 1983 as an intermediate range weapon with nuclear warhead to counter similar Soviet missiles. A comparatively inexpensive delivery missile, the BGM-109G has a terrain following guidance system permitting flight at altitudes low enough to avoid radar detection. Stored navigation electronics include an obstacle avoidance capability. TEL vehicles (Transporter/Erector/Launcher) each carrying four of these missiles could be dispersed in countryside locations in times of crisis. Two Tomahawk wings were established in the UK, at Greenham Common and Molesworth, where their presence was the subject of much protest by CND. With the signing of the Intermediate Force Treaty with the USSR in 1987 all Tomahawks were withdrawn from the UK and other European sites by August 1989. However, with conventional high explosive warhead or special materials, Tomahawks were fired from US Navy vessels during the Gulf War of 1990-91.

General Dynamics BGM-109G Tomahawk	
Engine	One 600 lb (2.66 kN) thrust Williams F107-WR-400 turbofan, with one 7,000 lb (31.14 kN) thrust solid-fuel rocket booster for launch.
Guidance	McDonnell Douglas inertial navigation system with Terrain Contour Matching.
Dimensions	Wing span 8ft 7 in (2.6 m). Length with booster 20 ft 6 in (6.25 m). Missile diameter 21 in (53 cm).
Weight	3,200 lb (1,454 kg) with booster.
Warhead	Originally thermonuclear, 80 kilotons explosive power.
Performance	Maximum speed 500 mph (800 kph). Flight altitude 10 ft to 500 ft (3 -150 m). Range 1,500 miles (2,413 km).

Both the Tomahawk and the TEL trailer in the American Air Museum were among several offered to museums in 1990 after secret equipment had been removed. The missile is actually an air-launched version while the transporter was used by the 501st Tactical Missile Wing at Greenham Common, although it was decommissioned at a USAF installation in Germany prior to delivery to Duxford in October 1992. DAS volunteers re-painted the transporter before positioning in the new building.

Aircraft engines that were significant in the development of American air power.

Curtiss OX-5

The first quantity production aircraft engine in the United States was designed by Glenn Curtiss and used to power his 'Jenny' trainer. Some 4,000 JN series aircraft were built for training pilots during the First World War, the model designation JN soon becoming Jenny in popular parlance. Curtiss employed an engineer at Sopwith's in England to draw up the design of the JN before it was put into production in America.

The example on display was acquired by the IWM in May 1937 from the R A Ford Depot at Kidbrooke, London. A plate attached to the engine states that it was reconstructed by Brazil Straker & Co Ltd of Fishponds, Bristol in 1917, and as such is believed to be the oldest surviving aero engine from the ancestry of manufacturers in Bristol.

Type	8 cylinder Vee, water cooled.
Power	90 bhp (67 kW) at 1,400 rpm.
Dimensions	Bore 4 in (102 mm). Stroke 5 in (127 mm). Capacity 503 cubic in (8.240 cc).
Weight	320 lb (145 kg).

Liberty V-12

The desire to acquire indigenous military aircraft during the First World War prompted the US government to sponsor the so-called Liberty aero engine for production by the automobile industry. Packard, responsible for the design, built with four other companies 17,935 up to the end of 1918. The 400 horse power rated, 12 cylinder water-cooled engine was used to power the licence built DH-4 aircraft, which in the summer of 1918 began to equip US Air Service squadrons in France, the only US-built aircraft to see operational use on the Western Front. The RAF used the Liberty engine in their DH9A bombers 1918-1933, serving in the UK, India, Iraq and Egypt.

The engine on display is on loan from the RAF Museum and was manufactured by the Lincoln Motor Company, Detroit, Michigan, in 1918.

Type	12-cylinder, 45 ° Vee, liquid cooled.
Power	400 hp (298 kW) at 1,750 rpm.
Dimensions	Bore 5in (127 mm). Stroke 7 in (177.8 mm). Capacity 1,649.92 cu in (26.3 litres).
Weight	790 lb (358 kg).

Pratt & Whitney R-1830 Twin Wasp

Considered one of the most reliable radial aero engines, the R-1830 was the military version of the twin-row radial developed from Pratt & Whitney's single-row nine cylinder R-1340 Wasp of 1927. Without increasing frontal area and causing greater drag, the Twin Wasp offered almost twice the power output. In fact, further developed the R-1830's rating was eventually increased to 1,200 hp during the dozen years it was in production. Most notable aircraft designs using Twin Wasps were the B-24 Liberator, Wildcat naval fighter, Catalina flying boat and the dependable C-47 Skytrain/Dakota series. More than 150,000 R-1830s were built.

Packard V-1650 Merlin

In 1940 Rolls-Royce arranged for Packard to licence produce the Merlin engine in America. These were used in some Australian, Canadian and US built aircraft types destined for RAF and Commonwealth air forces, and were also shipped to the UK for Lancaster bombers and Spitfire fighters in particular. In 1943 a more powerful version based on the British built 60 series Merlin with a two-stage supercharger was put into the new model Mustang. The result was a long-range fighter with a performance equal to or better than that of any enemy propeller driven fighter it was likely to encounter. Packard Merlin Mustangs achieved and maintained air superiority over most of Germany and enemy occupied Europe during the final year of hostilities. The Merlin originally displayed in the Museum was on loan from Mr Guy Black and sat on its original wood transit frame. This engine has since been replaced by a Merlin obtained from the Aircraft Restoration Company.

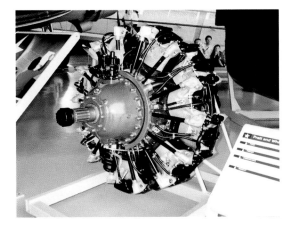

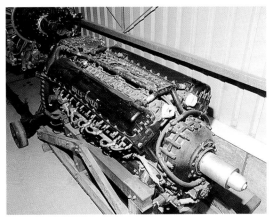

Type	14 cylinder, two-row air-cooled radial.
Power	1,200 hp (895 kW).
Dimensions	Bore 5½ in (139.5 mm). Stroke 5½ in (139.5 mm). Capacity 1,830 cubic inches (29.3 litres).
Weight	1,460 lb (662 kg).

Type	12-cylinder, 60 ° Vee, liquid cooled.
Power	Rated 1,650 hp (1,230 kW).
Dimensions	Bore 5.4 in (137.3 mm). Stroke 6 in (152.5 mm). Capacity 1,647 cu in (27 litres).
Weight	1,650 lbs (749 kg).

USAAF service vehicles that were a familiar sight on airfields in Britain 1942-1945.

108 US gallon 'Drop Tank'

Fighter aircraft engines, operating at high speed in a combat environment were heavy on fuel consumption thereby reducing range. Radius of action was a critical factor in US Eighth Air Force's urgent requirement for escort of its day bombers. Auxiliary jettisonable fuel tanks carried under fighters could extend range but a problem for the Americans was their need to operate at high altitudes where reduced atmospheric pressure prevented drawing fuel from these tanks. An ingenious method of pressurising the drop tanks was devised overcoming this problem and allowing Mustangs to provide support to any of the bombers' targets. Most of the drop tanks were made in the UK, largely from a plastic-bonded paper composition. The 108 US gallon tank of this type on display was donated to the IWM in 1984 by a former member of the manufacturer's staff.

Willys MB GP truck 'Jeep'

Without doubt the best known of all Second World War military vehicles, this ¼ ton General Purpose utility truck that became popularly known as the Jeep served the USAAF as a general runabout. Its four-wheel drive, rough terrain capability being particularly useful on the sod surface airfields and airstrips used by some Eighth and Ninth Air Force fighter groups. Nearly 640,000 Jeeps were built by Willys-Overland and Ford in four years and many were supplied to Allied forces. Jeeps survive in large numbers through post-war adaptation for a variety of commercial uses but by the end of the century purely as a novelty vehicle. The Jeep on display is on loan from the Duxford Aviation Society collection, purchased in 1996. Built in 1944, its military use has been traced to the Australian army. The DAS Motor Transport Section added licence-built parts from France to complete the restoration.

Type	108 US gallons (90 Imperial gallons/ 407 litres).
Construction	Impregnated compressed paper with internal gelatine lining.
Dimensions	Length 99½ in. 21½ in diameter.
Weight	52 lb empty.

Engine	60 bhp (44.7 kW) 4-cylinder Willys 'Go Devil' Petrol.
Dimensions	Length 11 ft 0¼ in (3.36 m). Width 5 ft 2 in (1,57 m). Height 4 ft 4 in (1.32m).
Weight	2,453 lb (1,113 kg).
Performance	Top speed 65 mph (105 kph). Fuel consumption 20 mpg (0.14 l/km). Range 300 miles (483 km).

Federal 605 C-2 breakdown truck

A special version of the US Army's 7½ ton three-axle wrecker truck was produced for the recovery of damaged or crashed aircraft. Fitted with a winch, swinging boom crane, support legs and a wheeled coupling for towing a semi-trailer, one of these wreckers was present at most Second World War airfields in Britain occupied by the USAAF. Their most common use was in recovering aircraft that had gone off the paved surface and become bogged down in soft ground. The Federal Motor Truck Company's plant was at Detroit, Michigan. On loan from Mr Voss, who acquired the vehicle and restored it at his Ampthill, Bedford garage, it was in a good state of preservation when received at Duxford and only required a new coat of paint which DAS members applied.

Crew	Four.
Engine	180 bhp (134 kW) 6-cylinder Hercules Model XD Petrol.
Dimensions	Length 33 ft 9½ in (10.30 m). Width 8 ft 0½ in (2.45 m). Height 10 ft 6 in (3.20 m).
Weight	27,500 lb (12,474 kg).
Performance	Top speed 30 mph (48 kph). Fuel consumption 3 mpg (0.94 l/km). Range 150 miles (241 km).

Certain supporting exhibits have no direct connection with US air power but are included as being evocative of the opposition during the Cold War and the Gulf War.

Section of the Berlin Wall

Epitomising the Cold War that pervaded Europe for more than forty years, the Berlin Wall erected by direction of the Soviets and East German government in 1961 stood until the latter lost power in 1989. The section on display is on loan to the IWM from the Royal Anglian Regiment Museum, a company of the Anglians having secured it while serving in the former British sector of Berlin.

Hunting JP-233 Airfield Denial Weapon

A British weapon originally developed for use against Warsaw Pact airfields in support of NATO strategy, the JP-233 dispensed high explosive for cratering runways and anti-personnel bomblets to halt their repair. Used by RAF Tornados against Iraq airfields during the Gulf War, delivery imposed great risk as the attacking aircraft flew at 200 feet and were vulnerable to ground fire. It is included in the American Air Museum to enhance cover of the Gulf War section. This example, donated by the Central Servicing Development Establishment at RAF Swanton Morley and presumably used at that station for developing maintenance procedures, came to Duxford in 1994.

Iraqi 1000 mm 'Babylon Supergun'

One of the 26 sections that made up the barrel of the famed 'biggest gun in the world' which Saddam Hussein was secretly building under the programme code name Babylon to threaten Iraq's neighbours in the late 1980s. It was cunningly devised to allow manufacture by foreign companies who would not be aware that the piece made was part of an artillery weapon. The 44 ton section displayed was apprehended by British customs in April 1990 before shipment overseas. The complete weapon was to be made up of 26 sections and was to have a 300 mile range firing one ton shells.

SA-2 surface-to-air missile

Notorious or famous, depending on one's viewpoint, 'SAMs' have been a useful air defence weapon in several military forces during the last forty years of the twentieth century. Brought into service by the Soviets in the mid-1950s and frequently upgraded, the SA-2 was supplied by the USSR to several nations within and outside its sphere of influence. Used with effect in the Vietnam conflict and the Arab-Israeli war of 1973 and also in the Gulf War during early 1991, SAMs were nevertheless slow and large enough to be observed by the crews of aircraft under attack and could often be outmanoeuvred. Radio/radar guided to target, SA-2s were vulnerable to the electronic counter measurers of which development usually kept ahead of Soviet attempts to counter. The American Air Museum example, a war trophy from Iraq, was donated by the Ministry of Defence. Little attention was necessary for its conservation at Duxford apart from a new coat of paint applied by DAS volunteers.

Engine	Solid fuelled rocket booster (first 4-5 seconds of flight). Liquid fuelled rocket sustainer (burns for 22 seconds).
Guidance	Radio command from ground radar tracking station.
Dimensions	Length 35 ft 2 in (10.72 m). Missile diameter 19¾ in (504 mm).
Weight	5,070 lb (2,300 kg).
Warhead	287 lb (130 kg) high explosive with proximity fuse. Burst radius 44 ft (13.5 m).
Performance	Top speed Mach 3.5 (approx 2,450 mph, 3,942 kph). Maximum range 31 miles (50 km). Maximum altitude 17 miles (27 km).

ZSU-23-4 self-propelled anti-aircraft gun

The ZSU-23-4 was developed during the 1960s to provide anti-aircraft support against low-level attacks on
Soviet ground forces. The four 23 mm cannon, having a
combined rate of fire of 800 rounds per minute, the ZSU-
23-4 was a formidable instrument of defence. This
armoured vehicle was supplied to Soviet allies and many
other military regimes and was used to good effect by
the Iraqi army during the Gulf War. The example in the
American Air Museum, captured during that conflict, first
arrived at Duxford in July 1991, being donated by the
Ministry of Defence in July 1991.

Crew	Four.
Engine	280 hp (208.8 kW) 6 cylinder V6R petrol.
Dimensions	Length 20 ft 8 in (6.30 m). Width 9 ft 8 in (2.95 m). Height with radar dish down 7 ft 4½ in (2.25 m).
Weight	30,870 lb (14,000 kg).
Armament	Four AZP 23 mm cannon.
Max vertical range	16,500 ft (5000 m).
Fire Control Radar	Optical reflector, ZAP-23 mechanical computing, 'GunDish'. Detection range 12½ miles (20 km).
Performance	Top speed 28 mph (45 kph). Fuel consumption 4 mpg (0.70 l/km). Range 162 miles (260 km).

Captured during the Gulf War and brought to the UK for an
investigative study, the SAM-2 was later given to the IWM. It was
delivered to Duxford on its special launch vehicle in 1992.
(DXP 94-29-57)

A formidable anti-aircraft weapon. The ZSU-23-4 photographed
on arrival at Duxford, 23 July 1991. (DUX 91-26-7)

Other attractions

From the raised level on entry, down the left-hand walk-
way and throughout the museum building, display
boards, photographs, captions and other graphics present the story of American air power from the earliest days
of powered flight to the end of the Twentieth Century.
Specific subjects covered are the decisive contribution
US air power made to Allied victory in the Second World
War, the importance of US productive capacity in this
respect, air power in the Korean and Vietnam conflicts
and its part as a deterrent factor in the Cold War, its use
in the Gulf War, the 'Special Relationship' and the US military presence in Britain. At the bottom of the left ramp
walkway the Gallery is entered. Named in honour of Lt
General 'Jimmy' Doolittle, one of the most famous names
in military aviation, who played a vitally important role in
launching the American Air Museum in Britain campaign
and in securing the wide support the Museum enjoys in
the United States. The Doolittle Gallery encompasses
exhibits relating to the Eighth and Ninth Air Forces which
at peak inventory when based in Britain constituted
more than half the combat strength of the USAAF. Busts
of the three wartime commanders of the Eighth Air
Force, Generals Spaatz, Eaker and Doolittle, acknowledge the contribution of these distinguished leaders.

A map table showing USAAF airfield stations in England with press-button facility to illuminate the various aircraft models deployed at each is based on a similar indicator board to that which proved the most popular fixture in the old Eighth Air Force Exhibition in Duxford's hangar No 3 annex. The story of the USAAF in Europe is told with an eight minute colour video documentary narrated by Charlton Heston. The video display unit for this is ingeniously sited in the rear of the B-24 Liberator nose section.

The Second World War in the Pacific, the Cold War and the Gulf War are also covered by interactive audio-visual units at appropriate locations in addition to innovative graphics.

The room under the entrance level floor is dedicated as the Georgia Frontiere Galley in acknowledgement of the special endeavours and generosity of US Appeal Board member Georgia Frontiere. This room contains several small displays. The two walls at the opposite ends of the gallery present name listings of all known Eighth Air Force combatants who lost their lives flying from Britain 1942-1945. A long rear wall display case and two smaller two-table top display cases hold the many artefacts and memorabilia donated by veterans or their families under the theme 'Americans In Britain'.

Visitors looking at the uniforms in the Georgia Frontiere Gallery, which include jackets worn by Generals Eaker and Doolittle. On each end of the show case there is a display of all Second World War Eighth Air Force combat group insignia based on that, funded by the 8th Air Force Memorial Museum Foundation, which graced the east wall of Hangar 4 for several years. (DX 97-1-834)

Visitors looking at the Roll of Honour listing the names of some 28,000 US airmen who lost their lives flying from Britain in the Second World War. (DX 97-1-838)

A popular exhibit, especially with youngsters, is the map table where airfields associated with different types of wartime aircraft can be illuminated. In the background is the B-24D Liberator nose section, the subject of a remarkable reconstruction programme. (DX CN 98-11-4)

These include uniforms – some flight jackets adorned with personal insignia, other personal equipment, log books, photographs, letters and a wide variety of items that reflect something of what life was like for these young men far from home. The two end panels of the long display case are adorned with 60 insignia of Eighth Air Force combat groups, a smaller scale version of the unique insignia display financed by the 8th Air Force Memorial Museum Foundation and positioned in Hangar 3 for several years. Another important acknowledgement in the Georgia Frontiere Gallery is the part played by US volunteers for the RAF before America entered the Second World War. Several hundred US citizens served in all RAF commands but the most publicised were those fighter pilots who made up the Eagle Squadrons.

The various themes presented in the American Air Museum are the work of Duxford's Exhibition Department staff under Stephen Woolford. Their efforts to have all story boards, graphics, models, captions and audio-visual equipment installed and completed by the date of the Royal opening was the most hastened and pressurised of all inputs. This was chiefly due to the delays in the building contractors finishing their work, which hindered what would have been a complex task in ideal circumstances and was made doubly difficult by dirt, dust and temporary obstructions.

A graphic reminder of the cost in airmen's lives are the 52 glass panels with over seven thousand engraved outlines of US aircraft missing in action while flying from Britain. (DUX CN 98-11-3)

Doyle E Larson, President of the United States Air Force Association, examines busts of Carl Spaatz and Ira Eaker. General Spaatz was the senior USAAF commander in the war against Nazi Germany and its allies. General Eaker headed the Eighth Air Force during its first crucial year of operations from Britain. (DX 98-29-3)

These men shouldered the major responsibility for the display within the building. Left to right: Steve Ridgeway, the exhibition designer, Martin Boswell, exhibition co-ordinator, and Stephen Woolford, head of interpretation.

Epilogue

The American Air Museum in Britain successfully combines an acknowledgement of the emergence and dominance of United States air power during the Twentieth Century with being a memorial to the 30,000 US airmen who lost their lives on active service in the United Kingdom during the Second World War. The memorial aspect is strikingly conveyed to the visitor approaching the entrance of the Museum by the glass sculpture 'Counting The Cost'. Lining the approach ramp are 52 large glass panels engraved with the plan outlines of 7,031 aircraft. These represent the total aircraft missing in action in operations from the United Kingdom by United States Army Air Forces and United States Navy during the Second World War. At a scale of 1:240 twelve types of aircraft used by the Eighth and Ninth Air Forces are arranged to show each group's losses, the group being the basic

operational unit of the USAAF. Several panels only have room for the losses of one individual group, some of those flying B-17s or B-24s from UK bases for two years or more having lost between 150 and 200 aircraft. This record does not include the many aircraft that crashed with loss of life in the UK while in the course of operations. 'Counting The Cost' is the work of young British sculptor Renato Niemis and was specially commissioned for the American Air Museum by the Imperial War Museum's Arts Record Committee and funded by private donation.

Apart from various prestigious awards gained by the American Air Museum its success can also be measured by the extraordinary effect on the number of visitors to Duxford. These rose by almost 50 % between the opening on 11 August 1997 and the end of the year, compared with the same period in the previous year. The increase in visitor numbers continued throughout the final two years of the century and this was undoubtedly due to the added attraction of the American Air Museum. US support continues for projects such as the B-24 Liberator restoration, forthcoming additions of the F-105, F-15 and SR-71 Blackbird, as well as the extension of the Georgia Frontiere Gallery which features memorabilia, personal items and highlights the everyday life of American airmen in Britain over the years.

The author wishes to acknowledge the generous assistance of Imperial War Museum Duxford officers, staff and associates in the compilation of this work, particularly Colette Byatt, Eleanor van Heyningen and Graham Thompson. Thanks are also due to Ken Ellis, George Pennick, Ian Mactaggart, Nigel Warnes and Bruce Robertson for additional material and advice.